G000058547

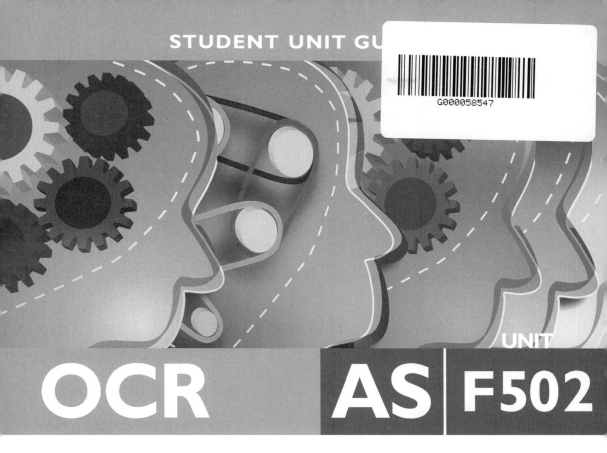

OCR

AS | F502

Critical
Thinking

Assessing and Developing Argument

Roy van den Brink-Budgen

Philip Allan Updates, an imprint of Hodder Education, an Hachette UK company, Market Place, Deddington, Oxfordshire OX15 0SE

Orders

Bookpoint Ltd, 130 Milton Park, Abingdon, Oxfordshire OX14 4SB
tel: 01235 827720
fax: 01235 400454
e-mail: uk.orders@bookpoint.co.uk
Lines are open 9.00 a.m.–5.00 p.m., Monday to Saturday, with a 24-hour message answering service. You can also order through the Philip Allan Updates website: www.philipallan.co.uk

ISBN 978-1-84489-554-0

First printed 2009
Impression number 5 4 3 2 1
Year 2014 2013 2012 2011 2010 2009

This guide has been written specifically to support students preparing for the OCR AS Critical Thinking Unit F502 examination. The content has been neither approved nor endorsed by OCR and remains the sole responsibility of the author.

Typeset by Phoenix Photosetting, Chatham, Kent
Printed by MPG Books, Bodmin

Hachette UK's policy is to use papers that are natural, renewable and recyclable products and made from wood grown in sustainable forests. The logging and manufacturing processes are expected to conform to the environmental regulations of the country of origin.

AS Critical Thinking

Contents

Introduction

■ ■ ■

Content Guidance

Producing arguments

■ ■ ■

Questions and Answers

Introduction

About this guide

This guide looks in detail at what is needed for good performance in the OCR AS F502 paper (Unit 2): Assessing and Developing Argument. It does this by considering the skills required and exploring how these skills are assessed by the sort of questions that you will find in this paper.

In the Content Guidance section all the skills are explained, demonstrated, and illustrated with examples.

In the Questions and Answers section you'll find these skills applied to sample exam questions. Sample answers are given — the good, the mediocre and the bad — with explanations of how an examiner would assess them.

Skills

Critical thinking is primarily concerned with how claims are used as the basis for drawing other claims, known as inferences, from them. These claims and inferences are normally referred to as *arguments*.

Unit F502 is concerned with the analysis, evaluation and production of such arguments. To do well in this unit, you therefore need to have the necessary skills to analyse, evaluate and produce arguments.

What are these skills?
- analysing the (explicit) structure of arguments
- identifying assumptions
- evaluating evidence
- evaluating reasoning
- identifying and explaining weaknesses (often called flaws) in argument
- identifying and evaluating analogies
- identifying and evaluating hypothetical arguments
- identifying, evaluating and applying principles
- understanding the significance of explanations
- recognising and producing counter-arguments
- producing further arguments

As with any set of skills, if you've got them and you've practised them enough, you should be at least reasonably competent. So keep this list of skills close by you. Tick off the skills you already have. Mark those that you're not so strong in, including those which you need to practise more.

The examiner and mark scheme

While you should have a reasonable level of competence if you've got the skills and you've practised them sufficiently, does this mean that the route to success in Unit F502 is now fully open?

Perhaps not: as well as having the skills, you need to understand what the examiner is looking for. So this book will help you to see how to keep an examiner happy.

Examiners will mark your examination papers according to an agreed mark scheme. For some questions there will only be one way to get full marks. With some other questions, however, the range of correct answers can be much broader. In these cases, when examiners come across alternative correct answers and unexpected approaches they will give marks that fairly reflect the relevant knowledge and skills demonstrated. This applies, for example, when you're asked for additional explanations for some evidence. So where does our examiner draw the line? At the point where the additional explanation is not plausible.

The examination

Let's just remind ourselves what the paper looks like.

Section A

This section consists of 15 multiple-choice questions. Each one carries only 1 mark.

Each of the questions contains a short passage followed by a question and then four possible responses. Sometimes one passage can support more than one question.

The questions all test the skills of analysis and evaluation.

Section B

The questions in this section are based on one or two passages. If two, then the first will be the longer of the two. But overall we're looking at about 400 words.

The questions will be mostly on evaluation of the reasoning in the passage(s). However, there will also be some analysis questions, such as:
- **What is the main conclusion?**
- **What is the intermediate conclusion?**
- **State a counter-assertion (counter-claim) given in paragraph *x*.**
- **In paragraph *x*, the author states '...'. Name the argument element and justify your answer.**
- **Identify the principle used in paragraph *x*.**
- **Identify the analogy used in paragraph *x*.**

The evaluation questions will be some of the following:

- **What is a weakness in the way in which the author uses evidence to support their argument in paragraph *x*?**
- **Give a strength or a weakness in the way the author uses evidence in paragraph *x*.**
- **Evaluate [a specific analogy] in terms of any strengths and weaknesses there are.**
- **The author sees the evidence in paragraph *x* in terms of *X* being caused by *Y*. What alternative explanation can you suggest for the relationship between *X* and *Y*?**
- **Name the flaw in the argument in paragraph *x* and explain why the reasoning is flawed.**
- **What is an implication of/implied by paragraph *x* and *y*?**

A chunkier question would be this:

- **Evaluate the reasoning in paragraphs *x* and *y*.**

With this question, you might be asked to consider a list of things, for example, 'flaws and appeals' (although, as we'll see later, there is no useful distinction between flaws and appeals — if an appeal is inappropriate, it's simply an example of a flaw).

You're also invited to look at the way the author has used 'examples'. We'll meet this issue later.

In addition, the paper might suggest that you look at 'hypothetical reasoning'. We'll be looking at this later too.

Things that you might want to consider under the general term 'other evaluation' include definitions and meaning, inconsistency (even contradiction), and problems with the evidence (problems of relevance, completeness, meaning, and so on).

Don't worry about all these things. Read on, and it will become clear how you can get the 30 marks available in Section B.

Section C

This is the section that asks you to produce arguments. Another 30 marks are on offer here. You may need to provide counter-reasoning, a counter-argument and a further argument. We'll look at how you should do these things in order to get the 30 marks.

Revision

For most of your subjects, you'll be encouraged to work out a scheme for revising the material that you need for the exam, so that by the time you do the exam you'll know enough to deal with the questions.

Critical thinking isn't like that. There isn't much you can do to revise. Critical thinking is essentially a set of skills, and since we get more skilful at something the more we practise it (think of music, dancing, juggling and so on), the best preparation for the exam is to do a lot of practising. You should look at arguments, good, bad or indifferent, and more specifically at how claims (including evidence) have been used in these arguments.

The next section (Content Guidance) will take you through all the skills needed for Unit F502. We look at the skills of analysis first. Having these skills will help you with all the sections on the exam paper.

Content Guidance

Unit F502 assesses the three main skill areas of critical thinking. These are analysis, evaluation, and production of argument.

The paper is divided into three parts, with the second and third parts each worth twice as many marks as the first. The first part of the paper provides 15 out of the 75 marks and is concerned with analysis and evaluation of argument. The second part provides 30 marks and also assesses your skills in analysis and evaluation, but much more the latter. Skills in producing argument are assessed in the third section of the paper, in which you will be asked to write further and counter-arguments (with, again, 30 marks available).

In this Content Guidance section we start with analysis. Skills related to analysis of argument are necessary for many of the multiple-choice questions that make up Section A and the early questions in Section B. The ability to analyse an argument is also necessary for successful production of arguments, so these skills run through the paper.

Analysis of arguments
Skills and terms

Skills in analysis of arguments are needed for both Section A and Section B. What skills are we looking at here?

- the ability to distinguish between the different parts of an argument: reasons, conclusions (intermediate and main), evidence and examples
- the ability to state assumptions that are made in arguments
- the ability to identify counter-claims/counter-assertions and counter-arguments
- the ability to identify principles
- the ability to identify analogies
- the ability to identify hypothetical reasoning

You will notice that OCR uses the term *argument element* for what we would normally call an *argument component* and for the familiar terms *reason, example, evidence, inter-mediate/main conclusion*, and *counter-claim/counter-assertion/counter-argument*. So when you see a question with the term *argument element* in it, just look for part of an argument such as these.

Notice that we are talking here about analysis, not evaluation. To be able to identify the structure of an argument is not the same as to judge whether it's good or not. Of course, if we're not able to analyse an argument, we can't do much evaluation, but the two skills are separate.

Analysis questions

What sort of analysis questions do we get in Unit F502? As we've seen, they occur in both Section A and Section B.

Section A

The following are typical analysis questions:

- **Which of the following is the *main conclusion* of the above argument?**
- **Which of the following is the *intermediate conclusion* of the above argument?**
- **What is the name given to the following *argument element* in the above passage?**
- **Which of the following is the best statement of the *counter-assertion* in the above argument?**
- **Which of the following is an *underlying assumption* of the above argument?**

Section B

The following are typical analysis questions:
- **State the main conclusion of the argument.**
- **State an/the intermediate conclusion of the argument.**
- **State the principle used in the argument/in paragraph** *x*.

Now that we're clear about what sort of analysis questions we need to practise, we should do some. We'll start by doing some simple analysis.

Reasons, conclusions and assumptions

Look at the following passage:

> Though a billion litres of bottled water were drunk in 2008, sales have fallen steeply since 2006. This is unsurprising. Only 9% of people in Britain believe tap water to be of poor quality. People are now less willing to pay at least 900 times the price of tap water to get a bottle of mineral water. The decline in the sales of bottled water will continue.

When we're doing analysis, the question we're really asking is, 'What's going on?' (or, if you prefer, 'What's occurring?'). This simple question takes us to the heart of a passage. It's asking what the author's doing and how they're doing it. So what *is* going on in this passage?

The author tells us that sales of water have fallen and then predicts that sales will continue to decline. That's the essence of the argument, and knowing this also gives us strong clues to its organisation.

Armed with these insights, let's look at the passage in more detail so that we can identify its structure.

What supports the main conclusion that 'the decline in the sales of bottled water will continue'? It is the claim that it's 'unsurprising' that 'sales have fallen steeply since 2006'. And why does the author think it's 'unsurprising'? The first reason is: 'Only 9% of people in Britain believe tap water to be of poor quality.' The second is: 'People are now less willing to pay at least 900 times the price of tap water to get a bottle of mineral water.'

So the argument consists of two reasons leading to an intermediate conclusion which is then used to draw the main conclusion. These two reasons are what are called independent reasons. In other words, each of them could be used separately to draw the conclusion.

As you can see, when you ask the question 'What's going on?' you make good progress in analysis.

If you were asked in the exam to identify the intermediate conclusion, it is of course the second sentence. But it would be helpful to unpack the word *this*, so that we can see that the intermediate conclusion is: 'The steep decline in sales of bottled water since 2006 is unsurprising' (or 'It is unsurprising that...').

Let's show the argument with its structure clear:

> R1: Only 9% of people in Britain believe tap water to be of poor quality.
>
> R2: People are now less willing to pay at least 900 times the price of tap water to get a bottle of mineral water.
>
> IC: It is unsurprising that, though a billion litres of bottled water were drunk in 2008, sales have fallen steeply since 2006.
>
> C: The decline in the sales of bottled water will continue.

Now that the structure has been laid bare, let's do some further analysis of the argument. What does the author of the argument have to assume?

(By the way, don't fret about the word 'underlying' in the multiple-choice questions about assumptions. The way the term is used, assumptions are never anything but 'underlying', so you can ignore it.)

You will notice that the question below is: 'Does the author have to assume any of these?' The words *have to* are central to the question. The question isn't 'Might they assume any of these?' or 'How probable is it that any of these are assumed?' The words *have to* remind us that assumptions are very demanding things. When we say that such and such is assumed in an argument, we're saying that the author cannot argue the way they do without including this claim in their reasoning. What we're really saying is, 'What is an additional reason that the author uses in their argument?' So let's return to the question.

> Does the author have to assume any of these?
> (a) Sales of bottled water in 2008 were lower than expected.
> (b) People drink more tap water than they do bottled water.
> (c) The price of bottled water won't come down substantially.
> (d) The percentage of people in Britain who see tap water as of good quality will increase.

Let's take them one by one.

Is (a) assumed? The author reports that sales of bottled water were low in 2008 compared to 2006, but they don't *have to* believe that this decline in sales was lower than expected. It would be consistent with their argument either way (sales lower/higher than expected). The fact that the sales had declined was enough for their argument.

Is (b) assumed? This seems to be consistent with the author's argument that people are switching away from bottled water to tap water, but it takes a step too far. The author could still argue the way they do if they believed the opposite. It could be, for example, that although people are switching to tap water, they still don't drink more of it than of bottled water.

Is (c) assumed? One of the two reasons used to draw the conclusion is that people are now less willing to pay so much for bottled water. The author, you will remember, predicts the continuing decline in sales of bottled water partly because of this price issue. So if the price came down substantially, the prediction would be a problem. As a result, the author does have to include (c) as an additional reason. In other words, (c) is assumed.

So is (d) also assumed? Although (d), if true, would strengthen the argument, it is not a necessary part of it. If the percentage of people seeing tap water as of good quality remained the same, the conclusion would still follow.

Counter-claims and counter-arguments

You will have come across arguments in which the author acknowledges or refers to an opposing position. They might do this in order to respond to this position or simply to note it. When the author merely refers to an opposing claim, we're looking at a counter-claim or counter-assertion. Here's an example:

> Though it is often claimed that modern Britain is a place where people are shown little respect, the reality is very different. In a recent report, 79% of people questioned said that everyone or most people showed them respect. We can see that all this talk of 'broken Britain' is so much nonsense.

The author refers to the claim that disrespect is common in Britain in order to provide the lead into their own argument which disputes the claim. The claim about respect is, in this argument, no more than that: it is a claim or assertion that goes against (or counter to) the author's own argument. In other words it is a counter-claim or counter-assertion.

Look at the next example:

> Some newspapers persist in giving the impression that support for the National Health Service has been declining. People, it is said, are not happy with the services offered by the NHS, so they are looking at using private medical care instead. However, the percentage of people satisfied with the NHS is now 51% (an increase of 17% since 1997). Dissatisfaction is at its lowest level since 1984 (only 30%, as opposed to 50% in 1984). The NHS is increasingly supported by the public.

In this argument, the author presents not just a counter-claim/-assertion but also an argument that presents the other side. This is the second sentence. As you can see, it is a simple argument:

> (R) People are not happy with the services offered by the NHS, (C) so they are looking at using private medical care instead.

Here we have, then, a counter-argument. We use the term when we find not just a reference to the side opposing the author's position, but this other side given in the form of an argument (with at least one reason used to draw at least one conclusion).

You will see that the first sentence is relevant to the counter-argument in the second but, though it is relevant, it is not part of this counter-argument. In relation to the whole argument, it is a counter-claim.

So let's look at the structure of the whole argument. We use the abbreviations CA for counter-argument and CC for counter-claim.

> (CC) Some newspapers persist in giving the impression that support for the National Health Service has been declining. (CA) People, it is said, are not happy with the services offered by the NHS, so they are looking at using private medical care instead. (R1) However, the percentage of people satisfied with the NHS is now 51% (an increase of 17% since 1997). (R2) Dissatisfaction is at its lowest level since 1984 (only 30%, as opposed to 50% in 1984). (C) The NHS is increasingly supported by the public.

You will have noticed that in both of the above examples, the author provides helpful signposts to indicate the presence of a counter-claim or counter-argument. These are words such as *however*, *but* and *alternatively*. It can be indicated, as in the first example, with phrases such as 'Though it is often claimed that'. Look out for this signposting, because it will help you see what's going on more quickly and easily.

Another thing to note is that a counter-claim or counter-argument tends to appear near the beginning of a short passage. This is not inevitable, but is very likely. This is because of the way in which we often argue. We would say, 'Some people believe X (because Y), but...' In other words, we set up the counter-position that we're about to knock down.

In longer passages, the counter-position could come later. This is because the author might well have all sorts of reasoning to present, and the counter-position is relevant to only part of it.

In the previous examples, we find the counter-position being included in the passage as something separate from the main argument. You will remember the point about words such as *however* and *but*. There are other passages in which the counter-position can appear in an argument but be absorbed into the argument, so to speak. Look at the next example:

> Arrests of girls and women have reached a record high level. This can be explained by females acting more and more like males (in behaviour such as drinking, being out late at night, and using violence). Thus we should stop

thinking that increases in female crime are a passing phase. The increase in female crime is going to be a growing problem.

You can see that the last but one sentence contains a counter-claim: 'increases in female crime are a passing phase'. The author rejects this with the reason given in the last sentence. The counter-claim is thus absorbed into the conclusion. Watch out for this type of counter-position.

Evidence and examples

When we're looking at the structure of an argument, we often find evidence and examples given as part of the overall argument. So do they play a part in the structure? This is a very slippery area, and trying to find our way through it results in all sorts of problems.

Look at the following brief argument:

Cows that are given names produce more milk than those that are treated as just one of a herd. Therefore, if farmers want to increase their milk yield, they should treat their cows as individuals.

What is the structure of this argument?

(R1) Cows that are given names produce more milk than those that are treated as just one of a herd. (C) Therefore, if farmers want to increase their milk yield, they should treat their cows as individuals.

It's simple because there's so little going on. A piece of evidence forms a reason to support an inference. You can't get any simpler than R → C.

What about the next argument?

In the nineteenth century, rich industrialists used to give money to set up local universities. For example, Bristol University received money from Mr Wills (tobacco) and Mr Fry (chocolate). It is unreasonable to expect the taxpayer to pay for most of the cost of higher education. We should encourage universities to raise money from rich individuals and companies.

What is the structure of this argument? The conclusion is obvious, but what are the reasons for it?

R1: In the nineteenth century, rich industrialists used to give money to set up local universities.

R2: It is unreasonable to expect the taxpayer to pay for most of the cost of higher education.

content guidance

The first reason is actually a piece of historical evidence. So what is the function of the second sentence in the passage? It obviously provides an example (or two, if you like) of the evidence. But what happens if it's not there? Not much. The evidence-claim that in the nineteenth century rich people gave money to universities stands or falls according to its historical truth. If this did happen, then there are presumably lots of examples. Giving the Bristol example does not make the argument stronger, does not *add* reasoning. Thus this second sentence is no more than an example.

However, examples can sometimes *also* supply reasons. Look at the next argument:

> In the nineteenth century, Bristol University received a lot of money from two rich industrialists, Mr Wills (tobacco) and Mr Fry (chocolate). Universities need a great deal of money for research. We should today encourage rich individuals and companies to give a lot of money to universities.

In this version, the example of Bristol University provides one of the reasons for the conclusion. You can check this by omitting the second reason:

> In the nineteenth century, Bristol University received a lot of money from two rich industrialists, Mr Wills (tobacco) and Mr Fry (chocolate). We should today encourage rich individuals and companies to give a lot of money to universities.

As you can see, the argument changes somewhat. It's an argument now about carrying on a tradition, rather than seeking to solve a problem.

So where are we with all this? Having looked at different arguments, we can see that there is a useful test we can use to judge whether evidence and examples are reasons or merely provide some support for reasons. In the following diagram, 'ev/ex' stands for evidence/example.

<pre>
          Can the specific conclusion still be drawn?
                    ↓   ↓
                   yes   no
                    ↓   ↓
          ev/ex not a reason   ev/ex is a reason
</pre>

At the start of this section, a list of skills used in analysing arguments was provided. Let's have a look at this list again and see what we have so far covered:

- the ability to distinguish between the different parts of an argument: reasons, conclusions (intermediate and main), evidence and examples
- the ability to state assumptions that are made in arguments
- the ability to identify counter-claims/counter-assertions and counter-arguments

We've still got the following to cover:

- the ability to identify principles
- the ability to identify analogies
- the ability to identify hypothetical reasoning

Identifying principles

Principles can be argued for, can be part of the explicit reasoning in an argument, or can be assumed in an argument. They can be just relevant to an argument. They can even be used as a reason to support another principle, as in this example:

> We should always seek to maximise people's welfare. So we should support policies which give people longer holidays.

Principles can be both positive and negative:

> We should give money to the homeless.
>
> We shouldn't eat meat.

But whether positive or negative, principles are guides to action, regardless of whether they are general or specific. The language of principles is that of *should, must, always* and so on, and their negative equivalents. In analysis questions, we're doing no more than finding them in an argument, so we're looking for statements that use this sort of language.

Identify the principle used in the following passage:

> A recent study has shown that the average teenager's iPod or digital music player contains almost 850 illegally copied songs. Each one of these illegally copied songs represents a loss of income for a large number of people (artist, company, producer, etc.). So it is good that internet providers are now going to start taking tougher action against this illegal downloading. It's no less than theft, however we might try to describe it. Since theft is always wrong, these illegal downloaders should be made to pay.

The essence of the argument is that illegal downloading is theft, and theft is always wrong, so it is good that internet providers are going to act. You will have spotted the principle: 'Theft is always wrong.' It had the language clue of *always*. (The author could have said, 'Theft is never justified/right/acceptable.')

In the next version, we pick up the argument halfway through:

> It is good that internet providers are now going to start taking tougher action against illegal downloading. It's no less than theft, however we might try to describe it. So these illegal downloaders should be made to pay.

In this version, we can see that the principle has been omitted. But it remains a necessary part of the argument to link 'It's no less than theft' and 'So these illegal downloaders should be made to pay.' In this version, then, the principle is assumed. (You can see that it must be, because without it the argument doesn't work.)

Identifying analogies

Analogies are a special type of argumentation. They are a way of using one thing's presumed similarity to another to argue from one thing to another. Here's an example:

> A source close to Simon Cowell said, 'He thinks Alexandra will be a big international star, if they get the music right. In many ways she is more versatile than Leona — she can really dance and there is a greater variety of things that she can do.'
>
> Asked if he was worried about the similarities between Leona and Alexandra, Cowell said, 'It is like asking would you want to sign up Whitney Houston when you already have Mariah Carey. Of course you would. There is room for more than one female singer.'

The analogy used by Simon Cowell is meant to provide support for his position that he is not worried about the similarities between Leona and Alexandra.

Questions on analogies will ask you to do a number of things, mostly concerned with evaluation. But you might be asked initially to *identify* an analogy. For example, you might well be pointed to a specific paragraph and asked to find the analogy in it.

So, where is the analogy in the following argument?

> A recent study has shown that the average teenager's iPod or digital music player contains almost 850 illegally copied songs. Each one of these illegally copied songs represents a loss of income for a large number of people (artist, company, producer, etc.). This is no less than theft, however we might try to describe it. It's just like stealing a CD from a shop, so it's about time young people started to realise that they're nothing but common thieves every time they download a track without paying for it.

Identifying an analogy is, at one level, pretty simple. You're always looking for a reference to a new scenario and for language such as *this is like, just as, this would be the same as*, and so on. So in this passage we find that the new scenario and the language used take us straight to the analogy: 'It's just like stealing a CD from a shop'.

But if you're asked to find an analogy, you need to do more than just identify the words. You need to unpack what is being compared. In this example, the comparison is between illegal downloading and stealing a CD. The author sees the act of illegally downloading a song as being the same as stealing a CD from a shop.

Interestingly, although the author uses the words *just like*, it needs to be remembered that in an analogy, the two things being compared can never be the same. They can only, at best, be very similar.

Identifying hypothetical reasoning

Hypothetical reasoning can play an important part in reasoning. It allows the author to present possibilities and connections. If we're just trying to identify some in an argument, then our task is pretty straightforward. (Hopefully, you've spotted hypothetical reasoning in the last sentence.) The most common form is *if...then* reasoning:

> To many older people, computer games are just things that young people play. This is no longer true. The average age of a computer game customer is around 30. It also needs to be recognised that the computer game industry is massively important for the world's economy. It should not be a surprise that the second biggest Japanese company (after Toyota, but ahead of Canon and Panasonic) is Nintendo. If the game industry continues to grow as it has been doing, then there will be few households in which games are not played.

In this example, the hypothetical is the conclusion. As you can see, it's in the straightforward form of *if...then*. But sometimes hypotheticals can be reversed:

> ...There will be few households in which games are not played, if the game industry continues to grow as it has been doing.

When the hypothetical is reversed, the meaning is of course the same. But watch out for such possible reversals.

You also need to be aware that the wording in hypothetical reasoning can sometimes vary from the normal *if...then* form:

> Were the number of old people to increase at an even faster rate than is the case today, the level of pensions would have to be reduced.

In this example, we have the equivalent of *if...then* but without any of the signposting words. So be alert to this variation. If you're asked to find hypothetical reasoning and you can't see the words *if* and *then*, you'll need to look for reasoning which has the same meaning, even though it uses different words. But you'll also have to realise that just because you've found the word *if* in a sentence, you may not necessarily have found some hypothetical reasoning.

> We need to act as if the number of old people will increase at a faster rate than at present.

In the above example there is something that looks like hypothetical reasoning in the sense 'if the number of old people will increase at a faster rate than present, then we need to act', but that's not what it is: it is saying that we *should* act in a particular way, rather than we should act 'if...'.

> We will never know what would have happened to species development if an asteroid hadn't hit the Earth 65 million years ago.

In the second example, the hypothetical 'if an asteroid...' isn't given as part of a piece of reasoning. It just presents an unknown scenario. Of course, you can see that this scenario could be turned into hypothetical reasoning:

> If an asteroid hadn't hit the Earth 65 million years ago, then the dinosaurs would still be dominating the planet.

So now we can both identify argument components (intermediate conclusions, principles, and so on) and use the language of argument analysis to label the components (example, evidence, counter-argument, and so on). We can tick off every item in our list of analysis skills:

- the ability to distinguish between the different parts of an argument: reasons, conclusions (intermediate and main), evidence and examples
- the ability to state assumptions that are made in arguments
- the ability to identify counter-claims/counter-assertions and counter-arguments
- the ability to identify principles
- the ability to identify analogies
- the ability to identify hypothetical reasoning

Evaluation of arguments

Skills

As with analysis, we can list the skills involved in evaluation:
- evaluating the significance of evidence
- evaluating reasoning: looking for strengths and weaknesses in argument
- evaluating analogies
- evaluating the use of principles
- implication, refutation and contradiction

Both Section A and Section B have questions on evaluation (especially Section B). In an important way, the skills of evaluation also run through the questions in Section C. When you write arguments, you need to be able to evaluate the reasoning you're using so that you can assess its relevance.

What are we doing when we're evaluating reasoning? Quite simply, we're looking at whether the inferences that have been drawn in an argument should have been drawn. We're asking the central questions, 'Does the reasoning sufficiently support the conclusion?' and then, 'If not, why not?'

Evaluating the significance of evidence

Familiar questions in this area are concerned with how an author has used evidence to argue in a particular way. This is an important area of critical thinking, because it goes to the very centre of what the subject is about — how drawing an inference from a claim (such as a piece of evidence) involves *giving the claim* (evidence) *a particular meaning*.

We'll look at an example to see how this works:

> About 10% of all US presidents (four out of 44) have been assassinated while in office. This death rate is about the same as that for street drug dealers. It is surprising, then, that so many people in the USA want to be president.

We take it, of course, that the figures are accurate. (They obviously are in the case of US presidents, and presumably are at least reasonably accurate in the case of street drug dealers.) Does the similarity in the figures tell us anything? Specifically, can the author of the argument legitimately draw their conclusion from them?

There are many things we could say. For example: you can't compare the experience of what's happened to 44 people over a period of 220 years with the death rate of thousands of people over a short period of time.

This really does get to the heart of the problem with the evidence. Though it takes the same thing and applies it to two groups, the two groups are different in all sorts of ways. The timescale of the US presidency goes from 1789 (George Washington) to the present. The timescale for street drug dealers will be much, much shorter. We're not told, but the figure referred to could well be an annual death rate. If so, then the comparison fails completely. The chances of a street drug dealer dying this year are presumably something like 10%. But there is probably not a 10% chance of the president being assassinated this year. We could add in further information, such as the fact that the last time a US president was assassinated was in 1963 (J. F. Kennedy), and the previous assassinations were in 1901, 1881 and 1865.

What we have done is to demonstrate that the significance of the evidence is not what the author gives it. We have shown, therefore, that the inference from it is hugely overdrawn. In fact, it is difficult to think of any useful inference that could be drawn from it.

The next example, however, is much less easy to dismiss:

> Four out of the past six US presidents have been left-handed. Furthermore, the current president is also left-handed. This shows that being left-handed is a distinct advantage for those who wish to become the US president.

Five out of seven of any group is a high proportion, especially when the proportion in the wider population is only one in ten (which is the rate of left-handedness). We could say the figure for left-handed US presidents is no more than coincidence, although again, the evidence seems to be too strong for that.

To evaluate the link between the evidence and the inference, what else would we need to know? Evidence of other heads of state? Evidence from other groups of successful people (heads of large companies, for example)? Think about this.

What sort of explanation would fit (with or without further evidence)? Here's one. It's from Jan van Strien, an expert in biological psychology at Erasmus University in Rotterdam:

> It is possible that left-handed politicians are more strong-willed because they've chosen not to conform to a right-handed world.

When we're considering questions involving the significance of evidence, we're often looking at the whole issue of cause and effect. And in looking at cause and effect, we're looking at explanations, which in turn leads us to envisage possible *alternative* explanations.

Read the following argument:

> Britain spends the highest amount on cosmetic surgery of any country in Europe. In 2006 this was £497m. The second highest was Italy with £158m. In fact, if we add up the total amount spent by the countries that were second, third (France), fourth (Germany) and fifth (Spain) in the league table of spending, this total is still less than the amount spent in Britain. This shows that British people are the vainest in Europe.

In this argument, the author takes the evidence to have only one explanation. This is that Britain has the highest level of spending on cosmetic surgery in Europe *because British people are the vainest in Europe*. In this way, then, vanity *causes* high expenditure. Our task is to consider alternative explanations.

It is interesting to note that in the 14 February 2008 edition of the *Metro* there was an article headed 'Vain UK's £1bn plastic surgery bill'. This article referred to the figure quoted above and also to the prediction that by 2011, the total will be £1.5bn. (So where does the £1bn figure come from? Is it a misleading average between the 2006 and 2011 figures?) However, we then read that 'while more people are going under the knife in Britain, procedures are generally more expensive here than abroad'. So straightaway we have another possible explanation, one that weakens the significance of the evidence in supporting the inference of British vanity.

What other explanations can we think of?
- Perhaps the *definition* of cosmetic surgery varies from country to country. For example, maybe Botox treatment is included in the figures in Britain but not in

other European countries. In addition, it is possible that figures for plastic surgery for people who've been injured or are disfigured are included in the British figures but not in those from other countries.

- Perhaps people come to Britain from abroad to have their cosmetic surgery done because there are *more* clinics here.
- Perhaps people come to Britain from abroad to have their cosmetic surgery done because the *quality* of the cosmetic surgery is very high.
- You might want to question the significance of the figures in relation to *population size*. This is often a useful route to alternative explanations. However, in this case, it doesn't work. The population of the UK is 59.8m; that of Italy is 58.1m, France is 60.7m, Germany is 82.7m, the only one noticeably lower than the UK being Spain with 43.4m.

As you can see, each different explanation creates a significant problem for the argument. What you might also have seen is that looking for alternative explanations highlights the assumption(s) that the author of an argument must make. To put it simply, the author of an argument that relies on a particular explanation must assume that 'there is no other explanation than...'. Thus, in this example, the author had to assume that the *only* explanation for the high level of spending on cosmetic surgery in Britain is the vanity of British people.

Looking for explanations shows us that we need to pay a lot of attention to the relationship between cause and effect in evidence we're given. It enables us to concentrate on the weakness (or flaw) in argument that is called *post hoc*. The full term is *post hoc ergo propter hoc* (a Latin phrase meaning 'after this, therefore because of this'), and it's useful to think of the whole phrase when we want to focus our attention on the evidence provided.

In the example we've just been looking at, the author is saying the explanation is *British vanity → higher spending on cosmetic surgery*. But, as we have seen, we can substitute other things for 'British vanity' to explain the effect. Perhaps we could muddle the relationship: *British vanity → higher spending on cosmetic surgery → British vanity*. This could work by thinking of more people having cosmetic surgery, so more people reflecting on how they look, so more people having cosmetic surgery.

If you want to avoid the Latin wording, you might prefer the English equivalents of *false cause, correlation not causation*, or *coincidental correlation*.

There is a similar construction with the term *cum hoc ergo propter hoc*. This means 'with this, therefore because of this'. It looks at two things that happen together and then sees a causal relationship between the two. In the above example, the author might say that British vanity and high levels of spending on cosmetic surgery exist at the same time, so there is a causal relationship between the two.

It needs to be stressed that both *post hoc* and *cum hoc* are flaws in argument only when the causal relationship is an inappropriate one. There are obviously many examples when we could say, without any problem, that one thing followed another, therefore the first caused the second. ('The car skidded out of control into a tree; the driver of the car was injured.' In this example, we are not going to puzzle over the causal relationship between the car's accident and the driver's injury.)

A much-fought-over argument is the cause of TB in cattle. Many farmers argue that badgers with TB infect their cattle. Because of this, they say, badgers should be culled. But you might be able to see the potential for a *post hoc* problem here. What is infecting what? If badgers have TB and cattle have TB, might the relationship be the other way round? A study published in 2006 argued that it was. When TB tests for cattle were halted during the foot-and-mouth disease outbreak in 2001, the level of TB in badgers went up. This would suggest that badgers caught TB from infected cattle (suspending the tests delayed removal of TB-affected cattle).

This again proves that considering alternative explanations helps us question how evidence is used and whether it is *sufficient* for an inference. When evidence is provided in an argument, it's seen by the author as at least contributing to their ability to draw the conclusion. They're saying that this evidence has sufficient significance for the argument.

Let's now focus on the sort of questions we need to ask (and answer) when we're looking at the significance of evidence:

- What significance has the author given the evidence? (What are they saying/assuming it *means*?)
- What other significance might there be? (What other explanations might there be which will give the evidence a different meaning?)
- How relevant is it, even if we accept the author's meaning?
- How relevant is it if we don't accept the author's meaning?
- Is it sufficient for the author's purpose?
- How is the evidence being used? (Is it the only evidence, the main evidence, one piece of evidence among many others?)

These questions will enable us to do all the evaluation necessary with the use of evidence. They should lead us to find both strengths and weaknesses.

What significance has the author given the evidence? (What are they saying/assuming it *means*?)

In asking and answering this question, we're doing what we did above — establishing what explanation the author is using for the evidence.

Look at the next example, noting in particular what Keith Vaz says:

In May 2008, someone was stabbed in a queue of customers for the computer game *Grand Theft Auto IV*. The MP Keith Vaz said, '*Grand Theft Auto IV* is a violent and nasty game, and it doesn't surprise me that some of those who play it behave in this way.' Sales of the game have exceeded 70 million worldwide.

Vaz sees the stabbing in the queue as being *caused* by playing *Grand Theft Auto IV*. This is the explanation he gives it. To him, the stabbing is *evidence* that the game is 'violent and nasty'. (Think back to *post hoc* reasoning or, more accurately, *cum hoc* reasoning, in that the queuing and the stabbing happen together.)

What other significance might there be? (What other explanations might there be which will give the evidence a different meaning?)

This should not be too difficult in this example. It could be that there is no link between the stabbing and the game. (After all, especially as the stabbing took place in the queue for the game, those involved are likely not yet to have played it.) Perhaps there was a disagreement/argument/incident that explains the stabbing which is not to do with the game itself.

How relevant is it, even if we accept the author's meaning?

Even if we accept the author's meaning, the relevance is limited by its being only one example of a stabbing. This point is reinforced by the sales figure of 'more than 70 million worldwide'. For there to be any great significance, we would need many more examples. (We could obviously provide many counter-examples in which people have not been stabbed or have not stabbed someone even though they've played the game. It might well be that you're one of them.) This takes us to the point about over-generalisation, which we'll pick up again later.

How relevant is it if we don't accept the author's meaning?

If we don't accept the author's significance of the stabbing event, then the connection between it and the playing of the game dissolves in front of us. It becomes quite simply irrelevant.

Is it sufficient for the author's purpose?

As we have seen, no. There are always problems in generalising from only one example. But the problem of over-generalisation is made worse by the fact that there is a big doubt about the causal relationship anyway.

How is the evidence being used? (Is it the only evidence, the main evidence, one piece of evidence among many others?)

The evidence is obviously the only one used. As we've just said above, this makes it a very weak support for the point that Keith Vaz wants to make.

We've spent some time looking at the evaluation of the significance of evidence. We're now moving on to look at the evaluation of reasoning in general.

Evaluating reasoning: looking for strengths and weaknesses

The title of this section serves to remind us that although we spend a lot of time looking at weaknesses in arguments, arguments can also be strong.

Arguments can have strength in a number of ways (just as they can have weakness in a number of ways):

- Strong arguments will have sufficient relevant reasoning to enable the author to draw a conclusion that fits with the reasoning.
- Strong arguments deal with counter-arguments (or counter-claims) by showing deficiencies in them and by demonstrating how the argument bats them away.
- Strong arguments move forward on as many fronts as necessary to make the conclusion fit well with the reasons.

We'll be returning in more detail to strong arguments when we look at how to produce your own arguments. But at this stage, you can see that by looking at the features of strong arguments we can also see the features of weak ones:

- Weak arguments will have insufficient relevant reasoning to enable the author to draw a conclusion that fits with the reasoning.
- Weak arguments fail to deal with counter-arguments (or counter-claims) — they don't show deficiencies in them or how the argument bats them away.
- Weak arguments do not move forward on as many fronts as necessary to make the conclusion fit well with the reasons.

Let's examine a strong argument before we look in more detail at some weaknesses in reasoning.

The Times of 22 October 2008 had an article entitled 'Daylight is precious. Let's stop wasting it.' It was by Stuart Hampson (Chairman of John Lewis 1993–2007). Try to have a look at the full article (search online for: Stuart Hampson The Times 22 October 2008).

Stuart Hampson argues that we should abandon the practice of setting our clocks to GMT in the winter and to GMT+1 hour in summer, and instead set them to GMT+1 in winter and GMT+2 in summer. Here's a summary of the content of the argument:

1 All time zones in the world are measured from the UK because the Greenwich (London) meridian is 'point zero'. (Hence the significance of GMT.)
2 Changing the clocks was introduced in 1916 to benefit farmers, but Britain is no longer an agricultural nation, so the working day has changed. (Typically, our day runs from 07.00 to 23.00, so the middle of the day is 15.00, not noon.)
3 It has been estimated that there would be 450 fewer deaths and serious injuries on our roads each year if we kept our clocks forward an hour. (This includes those of many children heading home from school in the dark.)

4 Crime would be reduced. (This is to do with a high proportion of crimes taking place at dusk.)

5 Old people would not be isolated behind their drawn curtains for as long on winter evenings.

6 More people would exercise after work, because it wouldn't be dark so early.

7 Businesses would benefit from having the same time zone as our European neighbours.

8 Farmers don't object to a change in the system. (See 2.)

9 A majority of people would prefer that we changed the system.

10 The demand for domestic, office and street lighting would go down, thus reducing energy bills and carbon emissions.

As you can see, Hampson's argument displays all the features of a strong one. He gives many different reasons, uses a lot of evidence, and deals with the counter-argument (about farmers).

You might well have seen the long list of weaknesses that you are expected to learn for the Unit assessment. There is little advantage in repeating it here, but a couple of points are worth noting. First, we shouldn't see this list of weaknesses as just a shopping list that will guide us through the shelves of the critical thinking super-market: I'm looking for a straw man (got one), a red herring (got one), an appeal to pity (can't see one), and so on. Weaknesses in argument are there aplenty. Read any letters page of a local newspaper or the comments page of an online newspaper: you'll easily spot them. Just know what a weakness is (the conclusion doesn't follow well enough from the reason) and be able to say why what you've just seen or heard is an example of one.

The second point is that a weakness is just that — a weakness. There is no point distinguishing between flaws and appeals. It is very puzzling to see it done, because it makes no sense. An inappropriate appeal is a flaw; when it's appropriate, it isn't a flaw (it's just a reason). It's as simple as that. It's no different from when a *post hoc* argument isn't flawed and when it is. Flawed appeals are flaws; appropriate appeals aren't flaws.

We're going to look at some of the flaws that you're likely to come across. We'll identify them and explain the specific feature of their weakness. This is just what you will have to do in the exam: identify the type of flaw and explain why it is such a flaw. (In the multiple-choice questions, you could be asked to find the weakness in an argument from a list of flaws.)

We've already met inappropriate *post hoc* reasoning. Whenever you find it, the expla-nation is always the same — the stated/assumed causal relationship between one thing and another can be doubted. Here's a simple example:

> In 2007, Ada Mason, then the oldest woman in Britain, died aged 111. Her granddaughter said that Ada attributed her long life to 'clean living' and a daily meal of bread and dripping with salt.

There you have the *post hoc* (or indeed *cum hoc*) argument: Ada Mason eats a daily meal of bread and dripping with salt and is 'clean living', *therefore* she lives until she is 111.

It should be pretty simple for you to explain the problem. With due respect to Ada Mason and her granddaughter, we can question the claimed causal relationship between long life and bread and dripping (with salt). There could be lots of other explanations (genetics, luck, and so on). (And just in case you decide to have salted bread and dripping every day for the next 90-odd years, remember the health warnings about fat and salt. Although adopting 'clean living' might be worth a try...)

We've already met the flaw of over-generalisation when looking at the Keith Vaz passage (see page 25). What he was doing there was taking one example of an incident (with a causal relationship problem) and generalising it to many more. It was in that way a double flaw. It would be like Keith Vaz explaining why bread and dripping with salt is to be commended for people in general on the basis of the Ada Mason evidence.

When does generalisation cross into over-generalisation? It's impossible to pin it down exactly. At the extremes (Ada Mason and Keith Vaz) it's easy, but whether the generalisation becomes acceptable depends on numbers, what's being generalised, over what timescale, and so on.

Here's an example, which refers to research from the Institute for Fiscal Studies:

> Research has shown that those born in August are significantly disadvantaged in education. This is because of the way the school year (and thus the exam system) is structured. Children whose birthdays are in August enter their school year up to almost one year behind their classmates. It used to be believed that children made up the difference as they got older, but this research suggests this is not necessarily so. For example, at the age of 16, August-born girls were 5.5 percentage points less likely than September-born girls to achieve 5 GCSEs (and August-born boys 6.1 percentage points less likely than those born in September). Exam boards should therefore take account of a student's birthday in giving out grades.

As you can see, the conclusion is based on evidence of students with birthdays in August and September. This isn't evidence based on a small survey. It is based on data supplied by the Department for Children, Schools and Families. In this way, the conclusion does fit with the evidence. It seems reasonable to look at ways of doing things differently. (Indeed the issue of how to deal with this problem is being investigated.)

But there is at least one generalisation happening. The argument is generalising from the past (the performance of students in a particular year) in order to make a recommendation about what should happen in the future. The argument is also generalising from these August-born young people to all August-born young people. Are these acceptable generalisations? Given the size of the database and the absence of any obvious indication that the group studied was in any way unusual, yes they are.

So can we infer that if you were born in August, your GCSE results won't be as good as those of your September-born friend? This is much more problematic. At the individual level, there's considerable room for differences. But if we were to say, 'If everything else is the same, except for your birthday, it is *likely* that your GCSE results won't be as good' (rather than they *won't* be as good), then this is based on a reasonable generalisation.

As you can see, we can generalise both ways. We can generalise from the big to the small (all August-born children to a few of them). We can also generalise from the small to the big (as in the Ada Mason and Keith Vaz examples). Both can involve problems. For example, generalising from the murders committed in London in a year to the number one could expect today can be a problem. So too is generalising from today's number of murders in London to the figure for the year. The way to approach these things, then, is to remember that the bigger the reach of the generalisation, the more potential there is for over-generalisation.

Note that you'll sometimes see over-generalisation referred to as 'hasty generalisation'. This is strange. 'Hasty' suggests, of course, 'speedy'. So a 'hasty generalisation' suggests that it's one done at speed. But this makes no sense. Someone could generalise at speed and still do something good with the evidence. Similarly, someone could spend hours fretting over a generalisation and still over-generalise.

We've looked in detail at two weaknesses: inappropriate *post hoc* reasoning and reasoning from over-generalisation. In both cases, the weakness comes from inadequate uses of evidence.

You'll find that most weaknesses can be seen as either flaws of *inadequate* evidence or flaws of *irrelevant* evidence. In *post hoc* and over-generalisation, the flaw occurs because the evidence is inadequate: it's not enough to establish the author's case. We'll look at flaws of irrelevant evidence shortly, but before we do, there's another flaw of inadequate evidence to consider: the slippery slope.

Slippery slopes

The term 'slippery slope' is nicely descriptive of this type of flawed argument. Here's an example (with a short slope). It's a letter written to the *Metro*:

> As a mother of two, I was shocked to see the image accompanying your article 'Too raunchy to be scene'. It left little to the imagination. Please remember that children have access to your newspaper. We do not need any more of our youth getting hooked on pornography after viewing free, easily accessible images like these.

(NB: the spelling of 'scene' is as in the original article, which was about sex scenes in films.)

The author of this letter, Annie from Manchester, worries that children who see 'free, easily accessible images' like the one published in an earlier edition of *Metro* will become 'hooked on pornography'.

There are two parts to the slippery slope here. The first is that children will start looking at pornography after they have seen images like the one in *Metro*. The second, a much steeper slope, is that they will then become 'hooked on pornography'.

This is a flaw of inadequate evidence because literally there is none at all. All we have are claims without anything to show why they are to be accepted. Is it really *Metro* today, addictive craving for pornography tomorrow?

So we can identify slippery slopes and we can explain why they are a problem: the author gives no (or insufficient) evidence to show that one thing leads to another (which leads to another...).

We're now going to look at flaws of *irrelevant* evidence. (Of course, irrelevant evidence is inadequate evidence, but the distinction remains a useful one.) There are many, and they're all types of 'red herring' argument: although the claims are irrelevant to the argument, they are designed to push you away from the real direction of the argument.

Ad hominem

A common type of irrelevant evidence argument is what you know as *ad hominem*. In this, the author directs their attack towards some (irrelevant) feature of their opponent rather than towards their opponent's argument itself.

Have a look at the next example:

> Thousands of people protested at the G20 summit in March 2009. They were a curious mixture of people from all sorts of different groups, with different agendas. Not only that, most of them looked as if they didn't bother to work. We should take no notice of the various demands that were being made.

The conclusion 'We should take no notice of the various demands that were being made' is supported by the second and third sentence. The claim in the second sentence might have some relevance to the conclusion if we take it that the existence of groups with different agendas means that we shouldn't take their demands seriously. But this is, at the very least, inadequate for the conclusion.

It's pretty clear, though, that the third sentence is an example of irrelevant evidence being used in an *ad hominem* way. The link between not working and what's being demanded is meant as a way of diminishing the significance of the demands. Quite simply, the author is attacking the people making the demands rather than dealing with the content of them.

Look at the next example:

> Thousands of people protested at the G20 summit in March 2009. They were very committed people who felt very strongly about issues such as poverty and climate change. The governments of the rich nations of the world should therefore act to change things.

This is also *ad hominem*, even though the author speaks well of the people putting forward an argument. But it's *ad hominem* for the same reason that the previous one is. (This type of argument is sometimes referred to as 'inverse *ad hominem*'.) The fact that the demonstrators are very committed people is not a relevant reason for governments to act on what they say.

So if you're asked to explain what you've identified as an *ad hominem* argument, you should always point to the irrelevance of a claim that's being made: the author says that X has the quality of Y but this Y is not relevant to arguing that Z should be the case.

Tu quoque

Another type of irrelevant evidence argument is what is called *tu quoque*. You will no doubt have come across this. It is, however, a somewhat confusing area. This is because there are different ways in which it is used. In its most common form, it's a type of *ad hominem* argument, because it is an argument form in which the person putting forward an argument is themselves attacked.

The following two extracts from an article in the *Daily Mail* of 3 April 2009 were part of a wider attack on the motives of those who demonstrated against the G20 summit:

> They profess concern about Third World poverty while dressing in designer hoodies and trainers knocked out by wage slaves paid a pittance in Far Eastern sweatshops.
>
> There are none so ludicrous as luvvies when it comes to saving the planet, as illustrated recently when Emma Thompson jetted off first class to the Oscars after addressing the camp set up to campaign against another runway at Heathrow.

In both cases, the author is attacking someone on the basis of inconsistency. In the first one, the demonstrators who are concerned about poverty in the developing world are seen as inconsistent because of what they wear. In the second, Emma Thompson is seen as inconsistent in speaking against the third Heathrow runway while allegedly being happy to use air transport.

Are these examples of *tu quoque*?

Yes, if the purpose of the author was, by showing they're inconsistent, to discredit the people who are putting forward an argument. It's in the form of, 'You're saying one thing but doing the opposite, therefore you (and consequently your position) are discredited.' In the first example, the author seeks to discredit the argument against reducing poverty in developing countries, and in the second, to discredit the argument against the third Heathrow runway. In both cases, the inconsistency would be irrelevant to an evaluation of the argument itself.

However, if the purpose were merely to show inconsistency, then the author's point would be relevant.

A variation of *tu quoque* is when someone argues that something apparently unacceptable that they've done or supported is acceptable on the basis that something else apparently unacceptable is done or supported by others. It's again concerned with consistency:

> Protesters at the G20 summit argued that smashing the property of the banks was acceptable because banks had smashed the lives of millions of ordinary people.

Here we have the familiar 'two wrongs make a right' flaw. (OCR has introduced its own version of this, with the term 'reasoning from wrong actions', but you'll find the familiar version more widely used.)

What makes the argument of the G20 protesters a problem is, of course, that the wrongness of one action does not enable one to defend another otherwise wrong action. It's an approach used by campaigners against the death penalty in the USA. Punishing a murder with premeditated state murder can't be justified: if murder is wrong, then it's always wrong.

Straw man

Another flaw of irrelevant evidence is the 'straw man' argument. This flaw occurs when someone gives a version of a counter-position that is distorted in order to show it as deliberately weak. In this way, the 'evidence' of the counter-position is irrelevant because it does not provide anything like an accurate version of the real version.

Here's another piece from the *Daily Mail*:

> Asking teenagers nicely to stop might be polite, but as any sane person knows by now, it is pointless pleading. Just as it is no good making empty threats. The missing link in knife crime — and across the criminal justice system — is the concept of punishment. The only way to deal with knife crime is to punish those directly responsible in a clear message which will deter others from falling into the teen-gang cycle of violence and retribution that so blights many inner-city areas.

This is part of an article which argues that punishments for knife crime should be much more severe than they are now. Can you spot the straw man in it?

It is right at the beginning. Those not advocating the use of greater punishments for people who carry knives are characterised as suggesting that we should ask 'teenagers nicely to stop' carrying knives. It is a deliberately weak position which the author sets up in order to knock it down (by reference to its rejection by 'any sane person').

A straw man is thus an example of the use of irrelevant evidence: the evidence of the opposing position is not given accurately, so what is given is irrelevant.

So if you have a question asking you to explain why what you've identified as a straw man is a weakness in the argument, your answer needs to stress that the author gives the counter-position in a deliberately weak way in order to more easily show the strength of their own argument. This inaccurately weak position does not strengthen the argument, because it is irrelevant evidence.

Inappropriate (and appropriate) appeals

Another example of weakness due to the irrelevance of evidence is the inappropriate appeal.

This can be a difficult area, because judging the appropriateness of an appeal is not always straightforward. For example, when is an **appeal to popularity** relevant?

> Fifty-five per cent of people in Britain believe in the existence of heaven and 70% believe that the human soul exists. This shows that science can't explain everything.

In this example, evidence of belief in the British population is used to draw an inference about science. Is the evidence relevant?

Not as it is presented, no. Whether or not science can explain everything is not dependent on what the public believes. It presumably can or it can't (although there are questions about whether the human brain can ever fully comprehend the nature of the universe — or universes).

What about the next example?

> In 1998, 38% of people in Britain said that they believed in horoscopes. Ten years later, the figure was only 22%. This shows that the British have become more sceptical about the claims of people such as Russell Grant.

In this example, the appeal to popularity is relevant. The decline in belief in astrology is relevant to the claim that people have become more sceptical.

Thus when you have identified an appeal to popularity, if you are explaining it as a weakness, you'll need to show that it's irrelevant evidence.

This approach will work with any of the appeals. Working out the relevance of an appeal is a task which requires us to look at the nature of the inference drawn from it. So when you see any appeal in an argument, you need to consider whether it is a relevant one.

Appeals to authority or expertise need to be judged in terms of whether the authority or expert is relevant in an argument. For example, an argument about the causes of an economic recession might well include a relevant appeal to the authority or expertise of an economist who has studied such causes.

It needs to be remembered that a good argument can include an emotional dimension. So an **appeal to emotion** (often given as pity) will be relevant in some situations:

> There has been a campaign to raise funds for the new children's hospice. The improvements in the nursing care of very sick children will be considerable. In addition, both the children and their families will be able to experience some joy and pleasure, even though there will also be sadness and, at times, despair. People should give generously to the campaign.

Is this not a useful argument? Though it appeals to emotion/pity, it does so in a context where this fits.

So in assessing the significance of an appeal in an argument, you need to consider the relevance of the appeal. We'll have a look at both relevant and irrelevant appeals in the following passages:

> Unemployment rates are not necessarily a guide to the popularity of a government. In the 1980s, the Conservatives remained in power (with increasing parliamentary majorities) even though their policies had massively increased unemployment. Even if unemployment rises, the government could still be re-elected.

You will have spotted an **appeal to history** in this. The claim that 'unemployment rates are not necessarily a guide to the popularity of a government' is supported by evidence from the 1980s. In this case, the appeal to history is relevant and therefore it lends support to the conclusion.

> Unemployment can be a tragedy for individuals and families. Those affected by it can lose their homes as a result of not being able to pay their rent or mortgage. Governments should do all they can to reduce unemployment.

The conclusion of this argument is drawn from an **appeal to pity**. Personal and family 'tragedy' is used as the only reason for governments to 'do all they can to reduce unemployment'. So is the appeal relevant or irrelevant evidence? It would depend on what is assumed in the argument. If the author assumes (as they seem to) that governments should try to minimise the amount of unhappiness in the country, then the appeal to pity is relevant. If they don't, then it isn't.

> The belief that capital punishment deters people from committing serious crime is a very old one. For thousands of years, the fear of death, especially a humiliating and possibly very painful one, was seen as the thing that would stop most people from breaking laws. This strong and persistent belief in the deterrent effect must therefore make any proposal to reintroduce capital punishment worth supporting.

The conclusion of this argument is drawn from one reason. The first sentence is the first reason and is, as you will have seen, an appeal to history (or tradition). It is an **appeal to a belief** (claim) with a long history. Is it relevant to this argument? No. The conclusion about the (assumed) strength of the deterrent effect of capital punishment cannot be drawn from the fact that a belief in this effect has a long history.

> In a recent survey of Nobel Prize winners in physiology and medicine, 92% said that experiments on animals are crucial to the development of many medical treatments. Therefore the people who protest against medical experiments on animals should be ignored. They clearly have nothing useful to say.

This is obviously an appeal to authority or expertise. In this argument, is the evidence of Nobel Prize winners relevant? This is a difficult one. Clearly, these Nobel Prize winners would be very significant scientists and it would be difficult to dismiss what they've got to say as irrelevant. The conclusion that 'people who protest against medical experiments on animals should be ignored' is drawn from the inference that 'they clearly have nothing useful to say'. This inference is drawn only from the evidence on the Nobel Prize winners. As a result, we can see that although the appeal to authority/expertise is certainly not irrelevant, it isn't enough for the author to reach that conclusion.

We have spent a lot of time looking at types of weakness in argument in which the weakness was due to either inadequate or irrelevant evidence. There is a third type, although it has features of the first. The two weaknesses that we're going to deal with next are: circular arguments and restricting the options.

Circular arguments

In circular arguments (sometimes called 'begging the question'), the conclusion essentially repeats the reason. In other words, there is no process of inference. The author concludes what they've already claimed:

> People should spend less and put more money aside each month. Thus people ought to save more than they do.

As you can see, the conclusion is no more than a restatement of the reason given for it. Why should people save more? Because they should.

What about the next one?

> Fish have the ability to feel pain in the same way as other animals. Therefore, when they are in pain, it will feel like what a dog, a cat or a person feels.

This has the same problem. 'Other animals' must include dogs, cats and people, so the conclusion has already been claimed in the reason.

You can test for a circular argument by simply reversing the sequence of reasoning:

> People ought to save more than they do. Thus people should spend less and put more money aside each month.

As you can see, it doesn't change anything. The argument is circular. It is clear why this weakness is one of inadequate evidence — there is *no* evidence given to enable the conclusion to be drawn.

Restricting the options

Restricting the options is a weakness in an argument if the options should not have been restricted. This might sound pretty obvious, but it needs to be remembered that there are times when there aren't many options (perhaps only two).

> The body under the floorboards is either that of the accused's wife or of someone else. Therefore it is very important that an early identification of the body is made.

Clearly the two options cover everything: either it is her or it isn't.

> Playing poker is either a game of skill or a game of luck. If it's a game of luck, then it's no different to gambling games such as roulette. However, if it's a game of skill, then it's closer to chess or darts. This distinction is important, because if it is a game of luck rather than skill, then it must be played only in licensed casinos. However, given that there are many professional poker players, this shows that it must be a game of skill. So it should be possible to play it anywhere.

This argument presents only two options: poker is a game of skill or it's a game of luck. What any poker player will tell you is that it is mostly skill, with some luck. The skill will come from bluffing, reading the other players' body language, making predictions, and so on. The luck comes from what cards are dealt. As a result, the argument ignores the third option, that poker is a game involving both skill and luck.

You can see how in this example the weakness came from the evidence being inadequate (if we take 'evidence' to mean claims). It didn't present us with enough evidence.

We need to remember that restricting the options can be a problem even when more than two options have been given:

> Binge-drinking among young people (especially among girls) is an increasing problem. The government can do one of three things: increase the price of alcohol significantly, make it more difficult for young people to get alcohol by restricting the places that can sell it, or increase the fines for retailers who sell it to under-age people. The government must therefore show it is serious about acting to reduce binge-drinking among the young by doing one of these things.

In this example, the options are restricted to three. But it's clear that there are lots more: for example, the government could have an advertising campaign aimed at young people and highlighting various unpleasant consequences of binge-drinking. In addition, of course, the government could do all three (or just two) of the listed options.

Having examined two of the five skills of evaluation listed earlier in this section (evaluating the significance of evidence and evaluating reasoning: looking for strengths and weaknesses in argument), we're now going to look at the three remaining ones:

- evaluating analogies
- evaluating the use of principles
- implication, refutation and contradiction

Analogies

In the section on analysis of argument, we explored how to identify analogies. You will remember that we need to look for both a change in scenario and specific types of language.

We'll focus now on how to evaluate the use of analogy in an argument. As you know, analogies cannot be judged against the yardstick of 'Are the two things/situations the same?' Of course they're not the same, or there wouldn't be an analogy. Rather, the author takes the two things or situations to be *sufficiently similar* for the analogy to be seen as supporting the reasoning (or indeed being the reason for the conclusion).

It's worth noting the term *disanalogy*. This can be seen as the opposite of analogy, in that you'll find one when the author says something like, 'X is nothing like Y, so whatever applies to Y doesn't apply to X.' An author would do this in order to emphasise the special nature of something. If people think that two things are similar (with consequences for an argument about one of them), then the author argues otherwise.

When we looked at identifying analogies, we used the following passage on illegal downloads:

> A recent study has shown that the average teenager's iPod or digital music player contains almost 850 illegally copied songs. Each one of these illegally copied songs represents a loss of income for a large number of people (artist, company, producer, etc.). This is no less than theft, however we might try to describe it. It's just like stealing a CD from a shop, so it's about time young people started to realise that they're nothing but common thieves every time they download a track without paying for it.

You will remember that we identified the analogy as the following: the author sees the act of illegally downloading a song as being the same as stealing a CD from a shop.

Just because the author uses the words *just like*, it doesn't mean that we can say, 'It isn't just like, so it can't be a good analogy.' We need to look at similarities and differences and then weigh them up.

What are the similarities?

In 2008, Kid Rock posted a video on YouTube attacking illegal downloading of music tracks. His message, summarised below, emphasises that such downloading is theft:

> I'm not going to miss the money. While you're about it, you need a new iPod, or a laptop? Steal it. Trust me, they won't notice it's gone. Want a new car? Just hot-wire a Toyota and drive it off the lot. They're foreign, so who cares? This is Kid Rock saying, 'It's okay to steal music and anything else you want to.'

Kid Rock's irony supports the author's analogy. Illegal downloading for him is straightforwardly theft, like any other theft (of iPods, laptops, cars and anything else).

In this way, we can see that by definition, illegal downloading is the same as other types of theft. The person who does it gets something without paying for it (and without ever intending to pay for it).

What are the differences?

Stealing a CD from a shop involves much more subterfuge. It isn't the sort of thing that you would do openly and frequently. There are probably CCTV cameras in the shop selling CDs, and also possibly security staff.

Downloading is presumably common practice with thousands of people. Stealing CDs from shops is presumably not common practice. (There's something of a *tu quoque* problem here.)

People who download tracks might well not know that it is illegal to do so. It would be difficult to find someone who doesn't know that stealing CDs is wrong.

Stealing CDs is a criminal offence, no question. Illegal downloading might well be dealt with as a civil law matter (though it can also be handled as a criminal offence).

Weighing things up

Numerically we have identified far more differences than similarities. However, the similarity is such a powerful one that we would probably decide that the analogy is a good one.

Principles

In the earlier section on analysis, we looked at how we can identify principles. We described them as general guides to action. Because they are general guides to action, they can be applied to a range of specific situations.

For example, the principle 'Cheating is always wrong' can be applied to taking exams, competing in sport, being faithful in marriage, and a lot of other situations. One way of evaluating the use of principles in arguments has therefore already shown itself: can the principle be used to apply to a wide range of situations?

In this example of 'Cheating is always wrong', what is it about being unfaithful to a partner that's the same as taking performance-enhancing drugs? Is the term *cheating* itself a problem, if it's used in a principle? In other words, is the term too vague or broad or disputed for a general principle?

You'll remember the principle that we found in the following argument:

> A recent study has shown that the average teenager's iPod or digital music player contains almost 850 illegally copied songs. Each one of these illegally copied songs represents a loss of income for a large number of people (artist, company, producer, etc.). So it is good that internet providers are now going to start taking tougher action against this illegal downloading. It's no less than theft, however we might try to describe it. Since theft is always wrong, these illegal downloaders should be made to pay.

The principle is 'Theft is always wrong.' How is the author using the word *theft* in this argument? They are using it to mean 'taking someone's property (in this example, income) by illegal means'. This is a straightforward use of the term.

It might be argued that 'theft' is by definition always wrong. But can you think of an exception in which 'theft' as such can be right? (Theft of a mad axeman's axe? Theft of a Nazi code machine in the Second World War?)

Another way of evaluating the use of principles in arguments is to see whether the author is consistent in how they apply a principle. Look at the next example:

> A national ID card system makes sense only if it enables the government to know what everybody's doing at any one time. Otherwise why have such a system? But for them to have this knowledge requires that we agree to constant monitoring. Clearly, the introduction of CCTV cameras in public places is a good thing both to deter crime and to help catch those who commit it. But the idea of further monitoring is unacceptable. Privacy cannot be sacrificed for security.

You will have spotted the author's principle at the end of the argument. And you will probably also have realised that the author is not consistent in applying this principle. The idea of ID cards is rejected on the grounds that they would require 'constant monitoring', which conflicts with the principle that 'privacy cannot be sacrificed for security'. However, the author commends the use of CCTV cameras on the grounds that they help to reduce crime. But if privacy cannot be sacrificed for security, then CCTV cameras cannot be justified either. The author's argument contains a blatant inconsistency.

Implication

> London's murder count reaches 90.

This was the headline of *thelondonpaper* on 28 July 2008.

As people grabbed the paper on their way to catch a train, they were meant to see this headline as telling them something beyond a message about numbers. This was, of course, that the number 90 was a cause for concern, indeed that it was alarming.

The reader was meant to draw something — an inference — from the claim. To read it and say, 'So?' was not the point. Neither, of course, were they expected to read it and ask, 'Is that all?'

We are looking here at implication. One way to think of implication is as a ripe apple on a tree. The apple hasn't been picked yet, but will be when you come along and take it. Once you've picked it, it becomes an inference. An unpicked apple has the potential to become one: it has 'implication' on it.

You might have heard the term used when people are arguing:

>   'I saw you looking at my boyfriend.'

>   'What are you implying by that?'

The implication could then be spelled out:

>   'That you fancy him.'

>   'What, him?'

So leaving them to sort that out, let's return to this claim:

> London's murder count reaches 90.

There's an interesting sting in the tail here. We've seen that the implication intended by the author of the headline was that this was a cause for concern. However, someone whose response was, 'Is that all?' would have been drawing a more accurate inference.

In a recent and very interesting study, it has been shown that although each murder is, in an important way, unpredictable, the overall number of murders is very predictable. The authors of the study have shown that in any one year, we would have expected 93 murders in London by 28 July. So the inference that should be drawn from 'London's murder count reaches 90' is either '2008 is looking to be a normal year, then' or 'Not too bad, then.'

(The study is 'London murders: a predictable pattern' by David Spiegelhalter and Arthur Barnett, published in the March 2009 issue of the journal *Significance*.)

So if you're asked, 'What is the author's implication in this passage?' you need to explore where the author's claims are heading. What does the author intend you to draw from what's been said? You're looking at the issue of consistency here: given the direction of the claim(s), what follows?

Refutation

If an author says that they have refuted someone else's argument, then they're saying they have demonstrated that it isn't true. This can be a very demanding requirement. For example, how could one contest the principle 'Theft is always wrong'?

However, refuting a factual claim is much more straightforward:

> The number of murders in London in 2008 was much higher than in previous years.

It would be possible, by looking at the evidence, to show whether or not this is true. But there are other claims in which refutation is hamstrung by the language used:

> Like a plague, murder by knife has taken London by storm.

This claim appears in an article on teenage knife crime on the website of Associated Content. The problem is that the expressions 'like a plague' and 'taken London by storm' can cause us to get caught up with the meaning of words. Has knife crime taken London 'by storm'? What does it mean anyway? How many knife crimes do there need to be to make them a 'plague'?

There is a relative of refutation which is very much like a playground bully. This is *repudiation*. Where refutation says, 'You can't claim that because here's some opposing evidence', repudiation just wades in and says, 'You can't claim that.'

Contradiction

This is used in critical thinking in the same way that it's used anywhere. An author is guilty of contradiction if they simultaneously make two contradictory claims.

> The country with the lowest infant mortality rate is Singapore, although it needs to be remembered that Iceland's rate is even lower.

It's obvious that if Singapore has the lowest rate, Iceland's can't be even lower.

You will remember the argument we looked at in the section on principles, in which the author praised the role of CCTV in crime reduction but also argued that 'privacy can't be sacrificed for security'. We noted that the author was inconsistent. But we could go further and say that the author was being contradictory. You can't hold both positions.

We've now dealt with the final three in our list of skills of evaluation:
- evaluating analogies
- evaluating the use of principles
- implication, refutation and contradiction

You should by now be able to deal with any questions on evaluation that are thrown at you.

Producing arguments
Skills

We have so far covered all that you need in order to analyse and evaluate arguments. The third skill is that of *producing* them.

This skill is the one needed in Section C of the paper. There are plenty of marks on offer — 30 in all — so it'll pay you to spend time and effort on these questions.

In a way, it's back to the skills of analysis. We've looked at how to unravel the structure of an argument into its components — reasons, conclusions, evidence/examples, counter-arguments and counter-claims/counter-assertions. All we have to do now is to take these argument components and build an argument using them.

Probably the best way to develop the skills of producing arguments is to write a lot of arguments. More specifically, you will benefit greatly from writing a wide variety of arguments which include many argument components.

You can try to do this everywhere you go. Just look at a claim that's made or think of one that could be made.

Here's an example. It's some evidence published in March 2009:

> Thirty-three per cent of British girls aged 15–16 said that they had been drunk in the past 30 days.

What can we do with this? Do we want to use this as a reason for a conclusion or as an intermediate conclusion? We could try both.

> (R) Thirty-three per cent of British girls aged 15–16 said that they had been drunk in the past 30 days. (C) Therefore parents should try to reduce their daughters' drinking.

> (R) Thirty-three per cent of British girls aged 15–16 said that they had been drunk in the past 30 days. (IC) So the campaigns showing the dangers of alcohol haven't worked very well with this age-group of girls. (C) Therefore a different approach is needed in order to make them see that drinking heavily can lead to all sorts of problems.

Let's now try using it as evidence as part of a wider argument:

> It's often argued that we ought to have a campaign to educate teenage girls about the dangers of alcohol because of their high levels of alcohol consumption. After all, 33% of British girls aged 15–16 said that they had been drunk in the past 30 days. However, the definition of 'being drunk' is likely to vary from person to person (is it 'being incapable' or 'feeling a bit merry'?). So it is very likely that the percentage of girls who were actually drunk is much lower than this evidence suggests. Therefore we don't need to educate teenage girls about the dangers of alcohol.

Look at what we've packed into this argument:

> (CA) It's often argued that we ought to have a campaign to educate teenage girls about the dangers of alcohol because of their high levels of alcohol consumption. (Evidence in support of CA) After all, 33% of British girls aged 15–16 said that they had been drunk in the past 30 days. However, (R) the definition of 'being drunk' is likely to vary from person to person (is it 'being incapable' or 'feeling a bit merry'?). (IC) So it is very likely that the percentage of girls who were actually drunk is much lower than this evidence suggests. (C) Therefore we don't need to educate teenage girls about the dangers of alcohol.

And all this from just one statistical claim!

Just think in terms of possibilities. How could a claim be used?

reason?

↑

evidence to support a reason? ← CLAIM → intermediate conclusion?

↓

counter-argument/counter-claim, counter-assertion?

Let's play around with another statistical claim:

> Twenty-eight per cent of teachers report often being bored by their work.

Think of some inferences that could be drawn from this:

> So people thinking of become teachers should think again.
>
> So more than a quarter of teachers don't enjoy their work.
>
> So schools need to look at how to motivate teachers better.

Then all sorts of things could be done with these inferences. We could use them as intermediate conclusions, as the conclusions of counter-arguments, as main conclusions.

Let's try using one of them as part of a counter-argument:

> It could be argued that young people who are interested in teaching should think again. This is because 28% of teachers report often being bored by their work. However, it is very likely that a fairly high proportion of people in other occupations are also often bored. There are no doubt bored architects, bored solicitors, and so on. So young people should not think that work is always going to be exciting. Much of work is routine, even dull (another catheter to insert, nurse). So teaching is probably no more or less boring than any other profession. Indeed it could be less boring than many. Therefore young people should not be put off teaching by this finding.

What a lot we've packed in.

A counter-argument:

> It could be argued that young people who are interested in teaching should think again. This is because 28% of teachers report often being bored by their work.

A reason (developed with examples) to support an intermediate conclusion:

> It is very likely that a fairly high proportion of people in other occupations are also often bored. There are no doubt bored architects, bored solicitors, and so on. So young people should not think that work is always going to be exciting.

Another reason supporting another intermediate conclusion:

> Much of work is routine, even dull (another catheter to insert, nurse). So teaching is probably no more or less boring than any other profession.

And yet another reason to support the intermediate conclusions on the way to the main conclusion:

> Indeed it could be less boring than many. Therefore young people should not be put off teaching by this finding.

We also allowed a little bit of humour in ('another catheter to insert, nurse'). Should you do this? In the hands of some supposed experts in critical thinking, the subject has a notable dullness. 'It's seven o'clock. I'm hungry. So it must be time for dinner.' (Yawn, yawn.) So why not include the occasional bit of humour? After all, the subject should be *vibrant* and *exciting*.

Get some practice by using any of the following as the starting point of an argument:

> More British households own two cars (27%) than have no car (23%).

> Eighty-five per cent of public toilets are cleaner than the average kitchen worktop in a British home. (So chop your onions in the public toilet on the way home?)

> It is predicted that by 2030, women will be the main earners in one in four households in Britain.

> In 1970, 80% of primary school children walked to school on their own. Today it is 9%.

Developing arguments in response to a conclusion

So far we've looked at developing argumentation from using statistical claims. But the normal task you're faced with in Section C is to develop argumentation in response to a given conclusion.

We can detail this task:

- You could be asked to write a counter-argument in response to the conclusion of the passage you were given.
- You could be asked to write a further argument (technically further reasoning) for the conclusion of the passage you were given.
- You could be asked to produce reasoning for or against a new conclusion that you will be given.
- You might even be asked to argue for or against a given principle.

In the third section of this book, we'll look at how such arguments will be assessed, but here we'll practise writing reasoning in response to a given conclusion.

When we were producing argumentation using a statistical claim as above, we were moving forwards. Here's a claim: what can be inferred from it? Now we're working backwards. Here's a conclusion: what reasoning can support it or oppose it?

We'll start with a conclusion and see what we can do with it:

> We should not allow children to be educated at home.

The obvious starting point with any exercise like this is to ask the question, 'Why (or why not)?' Asking this question takes us straight to the heart of the task. If something has been concluded, what reasons might lead us there (for a further argument) or lead us away from there (for a counter-argument)?

Let's think of some reasons why children should not be allowed to be educated at home. We'll just fire them off and then think about what we're going to do with them.

> Children need to be able to learn a wide range of subjects.
>
> Children need to get as many qualifications as possible.
>
> Children benefit from learning in the company of others.
>
> Most parents do not have the expertise to teach their children.
>
> Children need access to a range of facilities (such as laboratories) which cannot be available at home.
>
> Part of a child's education is to learn how to function with peers.
>
> Children benefit from interacting with many different adults, rather than just with parents.

And that's just by asking the question 'Why?' In answering this question, don't get caught up with the structure of the argument you're going to write. You're just coming up with material you can use in creating it. So don't think, 'I need to think of an intermediate conclusion now,' or, 'I need to think of the counter-argument now.' No, you don't. They'll emerge out of the products of your 'Why?' answers.

But now that we've got all these reasons to work with, we can look through our list and see if there are any that sit together to create lines of inference which will give us at least one intermediate conclusion.

What about these?

> Children need to be able to learn a wide range of subjects. So children need access to a range of facilities (such as laboratories) which cannot be available at home.

Already we can see that we've got a reason for an intermediate conclusion, so a structure can start emerging without us having fretted at all about creating one. Let's look further to see if we can do more.

> Children need to get as many qualifications as possible. So children need to be able to learn a wide range of subjects. So children need access to a range of facilities (such as laboratories) which cannot be available at home.

Wow! Two intermediate conclusions have emerged! Let's add what we've done so far to the conclusion that we started with:

> (R) Children need to get as many qualifications as possible. (IC1) So children need to be able to learn a wide range of subjects. (IC2) So children need access to a range of facilities (such as laboratories) which cannot be available at home. (C) Therefore we should not allow children to be educated at home.

Now what about the other things we came up with?

You'll see that if you look at the ones that are left, different lines of reasoning are now available to us. There are three that will fit together somehow, in that they're dealing with the same sort of issue:

> Children benefit from learning in the company of others.
>
> Part of a child's education is to learn how to function with peers.
>
> Children benefit from interacting with many different adults, rather than just with parents.

The first of these fits nicely as an inference from the other two:

> (R) Part of a child's education is to learn how to function with peers.
>
> (R) Children benefit from interacting with many different adults, rather than just with parents.
>
> (C) Children benefit from learning in the company of others.

So let's add this structured argument to the one we've already created:

> (R1) Children need to get as many qualifications as possible. (IC1) So children need to be able to learn a wide range of subjects. (IC2) So children need access to a range of facilities (such as laboratories) which cannot be available at home. (R2) Part of a child's education is to learn how to function with peers. (R3) Children benefit from interacting with many different adults, rather than just with parents. (IC3) Children benefit from learning in the company of others. (C) Therefore we should not allow children to be educated at home.

And what can we do with the one we've got left?

> Most parents do not have the expertise to teach their children.

Well this gives us yet another line of reasoning. As a result, it gives us a fourth reason.

> (R1) Children need to get as many qualifications as possible. (IC1) So children need to be able to learn a wide range of subjects. (IC2) So children need access to a range of facilities (such as laboratories) which cannot be available at home. (R2) Part of a child's education is to learn how to function with peers. (R3) Children benefit from interacting with many different adults, rather than just with parents. (IC3) Children benefit from learning in the company of others. (R4) Most parents do not have the expertise to teach their children. (C) Therefore we should not allow children to be educated at home.

Here's the structure of the argument:

$$
\begin{array}{ccc}
R1 & R2 \quad R3 & R4 \\
\downarrow & \downarrow & \downarrow \\
IC1 & IC3 & \downarrow \\
\downarrow & \downarrow & \downarrow \\
IC2 & \downarrow & \downarrow \\
\downarrow & \downarrow & \downarrow \\
\hline
& C &
\end{array}
$$

And all this from just firing off answers to the 'Why?' question!

Before we move on to do more, let's just slot in some connecting words and phrases so that the argument flows and thus reads well:

> It is clear that children need to get as many qualifications as possible. So they need to be able to learn a wide range of subjects. In consequence, children need access to a range of facilities (such as laboratories) which cannot be available at home. Furthermore, part of a child's education is to learn how to function with peers. In addition, children benefit from interacting with many different adults, rather than just with parents. So we can see that children benefit from learning in the company of others. There is also the point that most parents do not have the expertise to teach their children. Therefore we should not allow children to be educated at home.

It's looking good now. It's already going to light up the brain of even the glummest critical thinking examiner.

But we can do more. What about thinking of a counter-argument? What about some evidence or examples? What about a principle?

We know the counter-position has to be, 'We should allow children to be educated at home.' So all we need is at least one reason why this could be concluded:

> Some children have special talents that make it difficult for them to follow a normal school regime.

Let's do something with this one:

> It is the case that some children have special talents that make it difficult for them to follow a normal school regime. Examples are top junior tennis players and young actors. Thus, it is argued, we should allow children to be educated at home. However, it is clear that children need to get as many qualifications as possible... Therefore we should not allow children to be educated at home.

We've given only part of the argument, but this is to highlight the counter-argument we've created in which we've included a couple of examples.

Having done this with the counter-argument, we could look at adding some examples or evidence to the main argument. These appear in italics:

> It is the case that some children have special talents that make it difficult for them to follow a normal school regime. Examples are top junior tennis players and young actors. Thus, it is argued, we should allow children to be educated at home. However, it is clear that children need to get as many qualifications as possible. *(For most jobs or further courses, these will include Maths and English.)* So they need to be able to learn a wide range of subjects. In consequence, children need access to a range of facilities (such as laboratories) which cannot be available at home. Furthermore, part of a child's education is to learn how to function with peers. *(In a recent study, it has been shown that children who learn at home find it very difficult to cope when they go to university.)* In addition, children benefit from interacting with many different adults, rather than just with parents. So we can see that children benefit from learning in the company of others. There is also the point that most parents do not have the expertise to teach their children. Therefore we should not allow children to be educated at home.

Two pieces of evidence have been slotted in. The second mentions 'a recent study'. Referring vaguely to a recent study is a good way of bringing in evidence. It's very likely that you won't know any statistical evidence about the topic of the exam question. But don't worry — this is an assessment of critical thinking, not of general knowledge. If you don't know the details of a piece of evidence, making them sound plausible should be sufficient. Refer vaguely to 'a recent study' or 'parts of London', or whatever is appropriate. And of course, make sure that the evidence and examples you use are highly relevant to the argument.

So we've now got a counter-argument, four reasons, three intermediate conclusions, some examples, a piece of evidence, and a clearly stated main conclusion. We don't need any more, but we're on a roll, so let's add a principle. Can you think of any that might fit this argument?

> Parents should not be able to choose to act against the interests of their children.
>
> All children should learn how to interact with their peers.
>
> Education of children is the responsibility of the state rather than the private citizen.

You could have used any of these, but here's the second one put into a relevant place. You can see that it becomes a fifth reason:

> ...Furthermore, part of a child's education is to learn how to function with peers. (In a recent study, it has been shown that children who learn at home find it very difficult to cope when they go to university.) It needs to be stressed that all children should learn how to interact with their peers...

So from a given conclusion we made massive progress by asking the question 'Why?' The answers to the question gave us a large quantity of reasoning, which we were then able to sort into reasons and intermediate conclusions. It is quite simply the most productive way of getting an argument (counter or further) going.

Practise this method with any or all of the following:

> The sale of violent computer games should/should not be allowed.
>
> Farming has seriously damaged our environment.
>
> We should significantly reduce the number of guns that are available in the country.
>
> People who jeopardise their own health should not be treated on the NHS.

So we've spent some time looking at how arguments can be built up. We've produced a richly reasoned argument. But is it one that would satisfy the stern gaze of our examiner as he or she reads it? In the next section, we'll check to see how the marks for producing arguments are given out. We hope we'd have got all of them with what we've done here.

Questions
&
Answers

In the examination you will be given a resource booklet and the question paper. The resource booklet will contain either one or two documents which will be used for the questions in Section B and Section C of the paper.

Section A of the question paper will have 15 multiple-choice questions. Since each question is worth just 1 mark, this gives you 15 of the total of 75 marks of the paper. Section B will have questions on analysis and evaluation, giving a total of 30 marks. Section C will have questions on the production of arguments, giving you another 30 marks.

Section A

Multiple-choice questions
Strategies

You are advised to spend no more than 20 minutes on this part of the paper. Given that there are 90 minutes available in total, this would fit with its relative importance, in that it gives you about 20% of the total marks. You will also have noticed that it gives you only half of the marks available for each of the other two sections.

This last point is significant. The multiple-choice questions are an entirely separate part of the paper. There is no link between them and the questions in the other two sections. However, the questions in Section C are based on the material you have analysed and evaluated in Section B. This means that *when* you answer the Section A questions is worth thinking about. Indeed, you are expected to do Section A first (the question paper tells you 'on completion of Section A move directly on to Sections B and C'), but given that Section A is, if you like, free-floating, it would make no difference to your success in answering them if you did this section last. You don't want to be running out of time when you get to the 30-mark Section C, so if you're going to be short of time, it would be better if you had to rush Section A rather than Section C.

But it's not just a question of the number of marks. With the multiple-choice questions, all you have to do is select a box on the answer sheet. With Section C, you have to plan your answers and then write them up, paying attention to things like order and expression.

So, whenever you decide to answer these questions, how can you maximise your chances of getting them right? In one sense you could get some marks without doing any thinking at all. Say you put the same letter for every answer. You know that you'd get some marks, probably between 3 and 5. This is not the same as being random in spraying around A, B, C and D. That way you might never hit the target. But putting B for every answer would have given you 5 marks in a very recent paper, a third of the total marks.

Clearly we are not advocating doing this as a total strategy. But what we are saying is that faced with a shortage of time, you can get marks more easily in Section A than you can in Section C. There's another point too. Let's say that your brain goes into panic mode. We have all been there with critical thinking. You look at a question and you simply freeze up. You just can't get into it. You can't do it. Well, break out of the freeze by putting a B or... After all, it's only 1 mark.

Choosing the right answer

Having considered strategies for dealing with lack of time and brain-freezing, let's now look at the more important strategy of choosing the right answer by thinking it through.

How is it best to use your 20 minutes to answer 15 questions?
- Read the task.
- Read the passage.
- Look at the responses.

Though the question is laid out with the passage first, this is not the way to approach the question. There is little point in reading the passage without knowing why you're doing so. When you do know, you read it with a purpose. Sometimes a passage will support two or even three questions. In these cases, you should certainly read the passage with (at least) the first question in mind.

Having read the passage with the question in mind, you will very often have seen the answer before you even read the responses. For example, if you're asked to find the main conclusion, then you'll probably have already seen which bit of the passage it is as you read through it.

Unfortunately, there's one type of question that can be particularly troublesome. This is one that has a negative in it:

Which of the following is not...?

The reason why these questions are more difficult is that you have to slot out of one way of thinking and into another one. You're happily going through the questions looking for what is assumed, inferred, and so on, and then suddenly you're looking for something that isn't assumed, inferred, and so on. It's getting the brain to change gear from forward to backward, from yes to no. And all in the space of about a minute!

So how can you deal with this abrupt shift in thinking? By being careful to note the need for the shift, by slowing down just a little and then checking with yourself that the answer you've chosen is indeed *not* an assumption, *not* a principle used in the passage, and so on.

What sort of multiple-choice questions can there be?

You would always expect to see these — they are part of a long tradition of multiple-choice critical thinking questions:

Which of the following is an assumption of the argument?
(You may come across the full phrase 'underlying assumption', but don't worry about the word 'underlying': it's just an assumption that's being asked for.)

Which of the following is the main conclusion of the argument?

Which of the following is the best statement of the flaw in the argument?

Which of the following, if true, would most weaken (or strengthen) the argument?

You might also see some like these:

What is the name given to the following argument element in the argument?

Which of the following is a principle/appeal used in the argument?

Which of the following is a principle which would best support the conclusion of the argument?

Here's a claim: '…' How does this claim, if true, affect the argument?

Which of the following could be concluded from the passage?

Distractions

Let's just lift the lid on what is going on with these questions. If the question-setter knows their craft, then there will be elements in these questions designed to prevent all candidates getting all the answers right. Though there's sometimes a tendency for a parent to tell their children, 'You're all good' (at whatever it happens to be — singing, playing sport, acting, and so on), in the real world it would be a problem if all candidates were. The exam board would be horrified if everyone got 15 marks. Why? Because the questions then wouldn't be working. They have to discriminate in some way between different levels of ability.

So what does our question-setter do to avoid getting a phone call saying, 'You're fired'?

They try to distract enough candidates from the right answer.

- If they ask you to find the main conclusion, then they might put in an intermediate one, or use wording that has the look of an inference (*should*, *it is clear that...*), or include enough reasons for at least one of them to serve as a distracting response.
- If they ask you to find a flaw/weakness, then they should make the argument not obviously flawed in a way that hits you in the face. At least one wrong response should look as if it's stating something that might be wrong with the argument.
- If they ask you to find a principle, then they might want to include more than one statement in the argument that uses relevant language. If they don't, then you should be home and dry very quickly. For example, 'The number of people living in London has grown significantly' is obviously not a principle. The claim that 'it is necessary to explain the growth of London's population' has a 'must do' look to it, even though it isn't a principle. The claim 'London's population is getting too big' is perhaps heading off in the direction of a principle but hasn't got there. But the claim 'The people of London should not be disadvantaged by a fast-growing population' has at last delivered a principle.
- When they ask you to evaluate the significance of additional evidence, the question-writer has something up their sleeve. All the responses should be relevant

to the general topic of the argument. Some might have a neutral effect on the argument; some might go the opposite way to the question (weaken rather than strengthen, and vice versa). The simplest way to deal with this category is to put the responses in front of the conclusion: what does each one do? (Nothing/weakens/strengthens.)

- In questions on assumptions, there should be at least one wrong answer that goes in the direction of the argument without being needed by the argument. Consistency is not the same thing as being required for the reasoning to work.

Sample questions and answers

What follows are some multiple-choice questions with a detailed explanation of the correct answers (and why the incorrect ones are so).

Here are a couple of pretty easy questions. You would expect that the first one or two in the exam would be easy, as a sort of kind warm-up exercise.

(1)

> People buy bottled water when they are out and about. If they are discouraged from buying bottled water when they're out and about, then they'll buy cans of drink instead. There are many problems with such drinks (high sugar levels, additives, and so on). This shows that people ought to be encouraged to buy bottled water.

Which of the following is the main conclusion of the above argument?
   (a) There are many problems with cans of drink.
   (b) People buy bottled water when they're out.
   (c) If people are discouraged from buying bottled water, they'll buy cans of drink instead.
   (d) People ought to be encouraged to buy bottled water.

(2)

> Plastic bottles used for water are a massive problem. They are a big source of litter, and when they're not sent for recycling, they end up swelling landfill sites. In this country we are very lucky to have a supply of good clean water at the turn of a tap. Much of the world is not so lucky. So we should drink tap water rather than bottled water.

What is the following argument element in the above argument? 'Plastic bottles used for water are a massive problem.'
   (a) Reason
   (b) Intermediate conclusion
   (c) Evidence
   (d) Conclusion

(1) The correct answer is (d).

The structure of the argument is as follows:

> (R1) People buy bottled water when they are out and about. (IC) If they are discouraged from buying bottled water when they're out and about, then they'll buy cans of drink instead. (R2) There are many problems with such drinks (high sugar levels, additives, and so on). (C) This shows that people ought to be encouraged to buy bottled water.

$$R1$$
$$\downarrow$$
$$IC + R2$$
$$\downarrow$$
$$C$$

(2) The correct answer is (b).

The structure of the argument is as follows:

> (IC) Plastic bottles used for water are a massive problem. (R1) They are a big source of litter, and (R2) when they're not sent for recycling, they end up swelling landfill sites. (R3) In this country we are very lucky to have a supply of good clean water at the turn of a tap. (R4) Much of the world is not so lucky. (C) So we should drink tap water rather than bottled water.

$$R1 + R2$$
$$\downarrow$$
$$IC + R3 + R4$$
$$\downarrow$$
$$C$$

Here's a passage which supports two questions:

> The famous Nobel Prizes, awarded since 1901, remain the measure of scientific achievement. Of the 500 awards for science, 74 (15%) have gone to the UK. Given our population size, it's an impressive achievement that so many have been won. But since 1970 the percentage has declined. During the same time, the USA has dominated the awards. (It won about 60% of all science awards and in 2006 won all the awards for academic work.) Today it spends over twice as much of its national wealth on universities as we do. Since scientific discovery is heavily reliant on university spending, we need to spend more on our universities.

(3) Which of the following is the main conclusion of the above argument?
    (a) Scientific discovery is heavily reliant on university spending.
    (b) Nobel Prizes remain the measure of scientific achievement.
    (c) We need to spend more on our universities.

(d) **It's an impressive achievement that so many Nobel Prizes have been won by the UK.**

(4) **What is the following argument element in the above argument? 'Today it spends over twice as much of its national wealth on universities as we do.'**
   (a) **Reason**
   (b) **Counter-assertion**
   (c) **Evidence**
   (d) **Intermediate conclusion**

(3) The correct answer is (c).

(4) The correct answer is (a).

Here's the structure of the passage. You should have had no trouble finding the conclusion of this argument. Working out which bits are reasons and which no more than evidence or examples is what requires a lot of careful thought. The passage is annotated below and then discussed.

> (Ev) The famous Nobel Prizes, awarded since 1901, remain the measure of scientific achievement. (Ev) Of the 500 awards for science, 74 (15%) have gone to the UK. *(Inference from evidence)* Given our population size, it's an impressive achievement that so many have been won. But (R1) since 1970 the percentage has declined. (R2) During the same time, the USA has dominated the awards. (Ev) (It won about 60% of all science awards and (Ex) in 2006 won all the awards for academic work.) (R3) Today it spends over twice as much of its national wealth on universities as we do. Since (R4) scientific discovery is heavily reliant on university spending, (C) we need to spend more on our universities.

- **(Ev) The famous Nobel Prizes, awarded since 1901, remain the measure of scientific achievement.** This piece of evidence plays no part in the argument as such. It is what we would label 'scene-setting'. Without it, the argument is untouched. (Check to see.)

- **(Ev) Of the 500 awards for science, 74 (15%) have gone to the UK.** This evidence provides further scene-setting. Though it is more specifically focused on the thrust of the argument, the conclusion could still be drawn without it. This is because the argument is about what has been happening since 1970.

- **(Inference from evidence) Given our population size, it's an impressive achievement that so many have been won.** This is perhaps an odd one. The author draws an inference at this point, but it's not one that forms part of the actual reasoning of the argument. The reasoning starts with the next sentence.

- **But (R1) since 1970 the percentage has declined.** This is, of course, a piece of evidence. But it is evidence that supplies a reason for the conclusion. If we take it out, the contrast with the USA cannot be made and thus the argument is missing a crucial part. (Check what happens without it.)

- **(R2) During the same time, the USA has dominated the awards.** Again, this is a piece of evidence and, again, it's evidence which is essential for the argument. The conclusion is drawn by contrasting what happens in the UK and the USA.

- **(Ev) (It won about 60% of all science awards and (Ex) in 2006 won all the awards for academic work.)** Interestingly, we have here a sentence which consists of evidence and an example. Having been told that the USA has dominated the science awards since 1970, we don't need either the evidence or the example. They provide relevant detail (and perhaps add force to the strength of the reasoning) but are not necessary for the conclusion to follow.

- **(R3) Today it spends over twice as much of its national wealth on universities as we do.** Since the conclusion is about the need to spend more on our universities, this is an essential step in the reasoning. (Take it out and see what happens.)

- **(R4) Scientific discovery is heavily reliant on university spending.** You might have seen this as an intermediate conclusion, but it doesn't fit well like that. The previous reasons have not been sufficient to show this, so it works as the fourth reason.

- **(C) We need to spend more on our universities.** This looks like a conclusion and, of course, it *is* the conclusion.

Here's another passage that supports two questions:

UK births have risen since 2000 by about 10%. Despite the availability of screening for Down's syndrome, the number of Down's syndrome births has risen at a much greater rate during the same period, in fact by as much as 25%. This shows that more people are deciding not to abort Down's foetuses. This must then show that we have become a more caring society.

(5) **Which one of the following is NOT assumed in the above argument?**
   (a) **The effectiveness of screening for Down's syndrome has not declined since 2000.**
   (b) **Not aborting Down's syndrome foetuses is a sign of a caring society.**
   (c) **Before 2000, most foetuses with Down's syndrome were aborted.**
   (d) **The explanation for the increase in Down's syndrome babies is not due to something other than choice.**

(6) **Which one of the following is the best statement of the flaw in the above argument?**
   (a) **The author fails to consider an alternative explanation for the increase in Down's syndrome babies.**
   (b) **The rate of increase in births and that in the number of Down's syndrome babies cannot be compared.**
   (c) **The author fails to define what is meant by a 'caring society'.**

(d) The author gives insufficient evidence concerning the percentage of Down's syndrome births as part of the birth rate.

(5) The correct answer is (c).

The argument moves from the evidence concerning the relative increase in the number of Down's syndrome births to the inference that 'this shows that more people are deciding not to abort Down's babies'. This then serves as an intermediate conclusion from which the conclusion 'This must then show that we have become a more caring society' is drawn.

We need to work out what the author does *not* have to assume in this argument.

(a) is assumed. If the effectiveness of screening had declined, then this would provide an alternative explanation for the increase in Down's syndrome births. Since the author rules out any other explanation by drawing the intermediate conclusion, he or she has to assume (a).

(b) is assumed. This is needed to connect the intermediate conclusion with the main conclusion. Without it, the author could not draw the main conclusion.

(c) is not assumed. Though the author argues that fewer Down's syndrome foetuses are now aborted, he or she does not have to believe that 'most' were before 2000. He or she can be silent on this.

(d) is assumed. This is central to the author's argument. They must rule out any explanation other than people *choosing* not to abort Down's syndrome foetuses.

(6) The correct answer is (a).

From doing question (5), you can see how the argument is weakened by the author having to rule out any explanation other than the one about choice. This is captured in (a).

(b) is incorrect. There is no reason why the two cannot be compared. It is the inference that the author draws from this comparison that is the problem.

(c) is incorrect. Though the author doesn't define exactly what is meant by a 'caring society', he or she must include in the definition a concern for the existence of Down's syndrome babies. Not to have given it in specific terms is not in itself a flaw.

(d) is incorrect. Though the author doesn't give evidence on this percentage, he or she doesn't need to because this isn't the point. The author is concerned only with explaining why there has been a relatively greater increase in the number of Down's syndrome births.

Section B

Questions and answers

Section B provides a mixture of analysis and evaluation questions. Some of these are very predictable; others will be less so. We'll have a look at the predictable ones and a range of less predictable ones.

All the questions will be based on the passage or passages in the resource booklet. Here we'll use this passage:

> There has been a very serious decline in the numbers of shallow-water fish (such as cod) as a result of overfishing. People still want to eat fish, so the fishing industry must look at other sources, especially the deep waters of the Atlantic. Unfortunately, this has resulted in a catastrophic decline in the numbers of many of the species caught.
>
> Conservation measures will have to be put in place if these deep-sea fish are to survive. Research on five such species shows that numbers have declined by between 87% and 98%. This puts them in the category of 'critically endangered'. Many species could well disappear completely if the present trend continues. These are species that have been swimming in our oceans for hundreds of millions of years.
>
> The problem is emphasised by the fact that the decline in numbers happened in less than 20 years. We can't simply take whatever we want from the seas, as if we were robbers with a key to a bank. Deep-sea fish take a long time to reproduce and normally live for many years. Unfortunately their reproduction rate is very low. The average size of such fish also declined, with one species showing a 57% decline in average size. This is of particular concern, as large fish tend to produce more offspring than small ones.
>
> None of these facts has been taken into account by the fishing industry, which has fished the deep-sea species as if they were the fast-breeding sardine and herring. It is like culling elephants as if they reproduced at the same rate as rabbits.

The first question in section B is question 16, one of the highly predictable ones. It asks you to state the main conclusion in a passage. In the longer passages, you'd expect to find this near the beginning or near the end.

So what's the answer?

Conservation measures will have to be put in place if these deep-sea fish are to survive.

This would give you full marks. (The marks available for this question vary from 2 to 3, depending on factors such as the difficulty of finding the conclusion and the need to give marks to other questions.)

You can see that it reproduces exactly the way the conclusion appears in the text.

What might give fewer than full marks (but more than zero)? Something like this:

Conservation measures are needed for the survival of deep-sea fish.

In this version there is a paraphrasing of the conclusion which doesn't take it too far from the original but is still not quite accurate. Here is something to remember, then: paraphrasing might well be encouraged in some subjects to show that you've got that skill, but in the critical thinking papers it is very much discouraged. The question will ask you to 'state' the main conclusion, intermediate conclusion, and so on. So state it rather than paraphrase it.

One other word of warning. Don't think that you can use the conventional way of quoting something by shortening it through the use of '...', e.g.:

Conservation measures...these deep-sea fish are to survive.

The examiner is instructed to credit only the actual words that are used. This answer would be lucky to get the lowest mark available.

Another analysis question would be to state an/the intermediate conclusion. The same advice, of course, applies regarding accuracy in stating what's asked for.

Further analysis questions could include stating a principle used and naming what function part of the argument (the 'argument element' or component) has, e.g.:

State the principle used in the argument.

The answer is:

We can't simply take whatever we want from the seas.

Again we just need to find what's being asked for and then state it. So this answer would get full marks (up to 3). Marks are then reduced as we move away from accuracy for whatever reason:

We can't simply take whatever we want from the seas, as if we were robbers with a key to a bank.

This second answer loses a mark for adding something that is not part of the principle. The analogy that follows the principle is not part of it, so should not be included.

An even weaker answer is one that loses the accuracy of the original:

We shouldn't allow fishing in the sea.

A variation on *stating* the principle used in the argument would be a question asking you to *suggest* a principle that would support the argument (or a specified part of it). This is a more difficult question, since you're now looking for something that isn't there. But at least you can put this principle into your own words (as long as the principle you give is accurately expressed to fit the argument), for example:

We should not cause species to be endangered.

> This would be a larger principle than the specific one used in the argument but would certainly be consistent with the argument. It would get full marks.

> Here's a further example of an analysis question:

In paragraph 2, the author states: 'Many species could well disappear completely if the present trend continues.' Name the argument element used.

> In this type of question, you need to write very little. All that's needed is the term used for the specific argument component. (The answer could be a term such as explanation, example, evidence, reason, counter-argument, and so on.)

> The answer to this specific question is:

Hypothetical reason.

> A simple answer for the 1 mark that's available.

> These questions which ask you to name part of an argument are accompanied by a further question asking you to explain or justify your answer. The answer may seem obvious, perhaps so obvious that it's difficult to see what you're meant to say. Just writing, 'The reason is in the form of *if…then*' is accurate but insufficient. The examiner is expecting you to spell things out in detail:

It is a reason that includes a consequence ('many species could well disappear') that requires the condition ('if the present trend continues') to happen.

> That's what's needed. Obviously, the same spelling out is required if you have to justify any of the other argument components that you've been asked to name.

> An explanation could be justified like this:

It gives a reason why a decision to do X was taken when it was…

> For example, in the passage the final sentence of paragraph 1 is an explanation. Its function can be described in the following way:

This shows why taking fish from the deep waters of the Atlantic is something which must be very much controlled.

> An example could be justified like this:

It provides evidence of a specific case ('…') which illustrates the possible significance of the wider evidence ('…').

> The passage we're using contains a counter-argument ('People still want to eat fish, so the fishing industry must look at other sources'), so if we've been asked to justify why we've identified it as a counter-argument, then our answer would be as follows:

The main argument is in favour of putting conservation measures in place to protect fish, but this argument provides a reason why the fishing industry has to continue fishing.

A final type of analysis question concerns assumptions. You will remember that finding assumptions is nothing to do with evaluation. You are simply finding further reasons in the argument. Here's an example:

The author concludes that 'conservation measures will have to be put in place if these deep-sea fish are to survive'. What must they assume in order to argue this?

Here are two possible answers:

Conservation measures for deep-sea fish haven't already been put in place.

Conservation measures for deep-sea fish would work.

The marks are normally given on a 2, 1 and 0 basis. Two marks will be given for statements that are correct. By this, we mean statements that are sufficiently carefully expressed to be assumptions required by the argument.

Only 1 mark would be available for those statements that have some (but not much) inaccuracy, for example:

Conservation measures for fish haven't already been put in place.

Small as it might be, the omission of the words 'deep-sea' is crucial, because that's what the author's argument is about.

For zero, you'll need to be wrong:

People shouldn't eat fish.

Apart from the fact that this conflicts with the author's counter-argument (on which we don't know their position), they do not have to assume it in order to argue for the need for conservation measures for deep-sea fish.

We've so far looked at typical analysis questions. You will have seen that the watch-word with getting the full marks is *accuracy*. If you're told to 'state' something, then that's what you must do.

The rest of the questions in Section B are on evaluation. These will include questions on the evaluation of the significance of any evidence, on finding, naming and explaining flaws, on evaluating analogies, and on evaluating the reasoning.

Here's a question on analogies. You will have noticed that the passage we've been using has plenty of analogies. We'll look at two of these as sample questions.

In paragraph 3, the author uses the analogy that we can't just take what we want from the sea 'as if we were robbers with a key to a bank'. Make two points of assessment about this analogy.

In your question and answer booklet, you might then be presented with two sections to complete, each headed 'strength/weakness'. This is fine, although you might want to think in terms of similarities and dissimilarities here. After all, an analogy has strength to the extent that it has relevant similarities to what it's being compared to (and thus weakness to the extent that it has relevant differences).

Here are possible answers to this question:

Strengths

- The analogy captures the idea that people involved in deep-sea fishing take something that doesn't belong to them, just as bank robbers take something that doesn't belong to them.
- The analogy has the idea of an unacceptable consequence: the deep-sea fishing industry takes something which causes others to suffer. (These others might include people who care about this issue.) Similarly, bank robbers cause suffering by their actions.
- People who take the deep-sea fish are being irresponsible and not caring about others. Bank robbers do not care about those who are affected by their actions.
- In both scenarios there is short-term benefit at the expense of others (fish, other marine species, caring people, scientific researchers, and so on).

Weaknesses

- There is the point about legality. Even if robbers have a key to a bank, what they're doing is clearly illegal. What the deep-sea fishing industry is doing is presumably not illegal.
- Robbers in a bank are stealing other people's property; deep-sea fishing people are not, in the same sense, stealing others' property, in that deep-sea fish don't belong to anybody.
- It might be argued that there is a wider benefit from deep-sea fish being caught, in the sense that people eat the fish that are caught. Although one could argue that robbers will spend the stolen money on various things (thus benefiting the suppliers of these things), the money would have been used in some way by those from whom it was stolen. On the other hand, deep-sea fishing adds to the stock of things that can be used.

The answers above should each get good marks. As you can see, we have identified specific strengths and weaknesses in sufficient detail to gain the marks. Do remember that this exercise requires you to focus on the relationship between the analogy and the thing it is being compared with. As a result, any strength or weakness that you suggest must show this double relationship.

Answers attracting fewer marks might not show this double relationship:

People who take deep-sea fish are just taking the fish without any regard for the consequences.

This answer has a heavy hint of 'just like bank robbers', but this isn't developed.

Robbers in a bank are doing something illegal even though they've got a key.

Again, the possible connection with fishing has not been made, thus weakening the assessment.

Of course, there is also the 0 marks answer:

People who go fishing for deep-sea fish do it as a job and so get paid. Bank robbers don't rob banks for a job.

If you're asked to produce a judgement on the analogy, then you would again need to look at how the two parts can be compared:

The analogy suffers from the problem of the difference in the legality of the two things. Though there are some useful similarities, this problem of legality (and ownership) does reduce the power of the analogy. To rescue it, we would have to see the two situations as involving selfish acts without regard to the consequences of what's done.

There will be various questions on the evaluation of any evidence used. Here's a typical question:

In paragraph 1, the author uses evidence that X% of people believe Y. Explain one weakness or strength in the use of this evidence.

If we apply this to our passage, we could have the following question:

In paragraph 2, the author uses evidence of research on five deep-sea species of fish which 'shows that numbers have declined by between 87% and 98%.' Explain one strength or one weakness in the use of this evidence.

One weakness is that we don't know how typical the five species are: it could be that they're the ones most likely to be caught.

Here we have an answer that will get full (2) marks. Not only is a point of evaluation made about not knowing how typical these species are, but there's also an explanation of why they might not be typical.

The next answer gives a strength in the evidence. It also gets the full marks as a result of its developed explanation:

The very high percentage in each case is significant because it's unlikely that other deep-sea fish are not also suffering decline, in that they're unlikely to be able to escape the nets used by the fishing boats.

An answer that doesn't provide any development could attract just 1 mark:

Some species might not have declined so much.

As stated earlier, you might have one or two documents which are used for the questions. Here, then, is a second document:

The entire ecosystem of the world's seas could collapse by 2050. There is no future for the world's coral reefs other than their preservation in huge artificial aquaria or their complete destruction. Only urgent action taken very soon can

> prevent this collapse from happening. One of the major causes of the problem for the ecosystem of the seas is overfishing. The Black Sea has shown what happens. Large fish disappeared from this sea by the 1970s. Twenty years later, the smaller ones had gone. This is the fate that will soon await all the world's seas, unless large-scale action is taken. We must remember that fish are a crucial part of the ecosystem of the seas and therefore of the world. We must stop thinking of fish as a food product that can simply be collected for our plates.

You are very likely to have a question asking you to name a particular flaw in the material you're given and then to explain why this part of the reasoning is flawed. Here's an example:

The reasoning about coral reefs contains a flaw. Name the flaw and explain the weakness in this reasoning.

Restriction of options.

The author gives only two options for the future of coral reefs, which is a problem given that they argue that complete destruction could be prevented if we take urgent action. Presumably, if we take this urgent action there could be other scenarios, such as marine reserves to protect the reefs.

> We get 1 mark for correctly naming the flaw. (We could have put 'false dilemma' instead.)

> We get 2 marks for explaining why this is an example of restriction of options.

> A 1-mark answer gives much less detail:

The author gives only two things that could happen to coral reefs, but there could be more.

> You are also very likely to have a question which asks you to evaluate a paragraph of reasoning. In doing this you might be asked to give a number (say, two) of strengths or weaknesses or to do specific things such as referring to flaws, to inappropriate appeals, to the way in which evidence is used, and so on. Here's an example:

Evaluate the reasoning in the second document. You should refer to at least two strengths or weaknesses.

> The way to get marks in questions set out like this is to make sure that you state what is a strength or weakness, explain why it is, and then develop this explanation (especially referring to the passage). For example:

The author argues that 'overfishing' is 'one of the major causes of the problem for the ecosystem of the seas'. The rest of the argument focuses entirely on fishing as a problem. However, we need to know about these other causes (such as pollution, presumably). Since the author doesn't say anything about these other causes, the conclusion addresses only part of the problem. Even if we changed our attitude to fish, it is likely that there would still be problems for the seas.

If the Black Sea is somehow typical of other seas and of the world's oceans, then this example can be used to show what will soon happen. The short timescale in which the Black Sea collapsed emphasises the problem that overfishing cannot be sustained.

An alternative treatment of the Black Sea example could show it as a weakness:

It could be that the Black Sea is not typical of the world's seas and oceans. Perhaps it is more polluted than the global oceans; perhaps it has been particularly overfished, to a much greater degree than other seas and oceans. In this way, we could see this example as being not very relevant to the wider problem. (If you had known this, you could have mentioned that the Black Sea isn't typical of the oceans and open seas, because it's largely a landlocked sea. But you didn't need to know this to question whether it's typical, as here, in a hypothetical form.)

You can see that we have identified a strength or weakness in the text, explained why it was so, and developed this explanation sufficiently. Weaker answers would not provide so much development:

We're told only about one of the causes of the problem. Perhaps overfishing isn't the biggest problem.

Section B comes to an end, having delivered 30 marks. It asks, as we have seen, a mixture of analysis and evaluation questions. Section C now comes along with a further 30 marks for (normally) three or four 'production of argument' questions.

Production of arguments

The questions in this section fall into two categories. The first is those that ask you to develop a position that's given or to indicate problems that a position might create. The second, and by far the bigger of the two in terms of marks, asks you to produce developed arguments.

The first one or two questions will provide 6 of the 30 marks. They can vary in their format but at root they're asking you to develop part of the existing material.

The author of the second document argues that the ecosystems of the world's seas could collapse by 2050 'unless large-scale action is taken'. Give one detailed example of problems that there could be in getting this 'large-scale action' taken.

We give two answers:

The author doesn't explain what this large-scale action should be and how it could be achieved. Presumably it will involve many (if not, all) countries agreeing to significantly reduce their levels of fishing. Perhaps there will have to be no fishing at all in some parts of the world. It is difficult to see this agreement being reached.

There would be huge problems in getting agreement on large-scale action (as there is with climate change policies), but even if it was agreed, it would be very difficult to get it controlled. The world's oceans are so big that we couldn't patrol all of them to ensure that the restrictions were being adhered to.

We're normally looking at 3 marks for an answer in this part of Section C. (Three marks given for each answer, with either two answers for one question or one answer for each of two questions.)

How do our answers rate regarding the 3 marks available? They should, of course, each get all of them. They explain clearly what the problem is (getting agreement and policing it) and give plenty of details to show why it is a problem. Lower marks would therefore be given for less clear and/or less developed answers:

It would be a problem getting countries to agree because there are lots of them.

It would be a problem working out how to stop people still fishing.

Now we need to look at the final two questions. Each of these carries 12 marks, so, as we discussed when we were looking at the multiple-choice questions, you need to make sure that you have enough time to do these as well as possible.

The most likely task that you'll be given in these two questions is to write a further argument and/or a counter-argument. A further argument is an additional one in support of an existing argument, using additional reasons to the ones already used: here is an argument in support of X, now give some additional reasons in support of X. A counter-argument, as you already know, is an argument against an existing one.

However, you could find yourself being presented with a claim which has the look of a conclusion and being asked to write an argument which either supports or challenges the claim. This will be a claim which is in the general area of the material you will have been given.

Let's have a look at how the marks will be awarded for writing arguments.

The mark scheme is based on five levels of performance. These levels attract marks as follows:

> 10–12 marks
> 7–9 marks
> 4–6 marks
> 1–3 marks
> 0 marks

You will, of course, be mostly (only) interested in what the top band of marks is awarded for. (After all, that's the one we're aiming for.)

Before we do this, it will be useful to remind ourselves what the instructions on the paper tell you to do:

Marks will be given for a well structured and developed argument. You should include at least three reasons, a well supported intermediate conclusion and a main conclusion. Your argument may also contain other argument elements.

In addition, you're likely to find this:

You may use information and ideas from the passage, but you must use them to form a new argument. No credit will be given for repeating the reasoning in the passage.

Let's compare this with what the examiner is told to look for in giving a top-level mark:

Candidates present their own relevant argument with a clear structure where the conclusion is supported by at least three reasons and at least one properly supported intermediate conclusion. The argument is convincing and may rely on only one or two reasonable assumptions. The argument may also contain relevant argument elements, e.g. evidence/examples, counter-assertion. The main conclusion is precisely and correctly stated. Grammar, spelling and punctuation are very good: errors are few, if any.

Let's look first of all at the similarities between the two versions:
- well structured/clearly structured argument
- at least three reasons
- a well supported/properly supported intermediate conclusion
- a main conclusion

Given that the examiner is looking at the mark scheme rather than the question paper when they're marking your script, it makes most sense to do what they're looking for rather than what you've been asked to do. So it seems to be a good policy to go for more than one intermediate conclusion.

Is there a difference between a well structured and a clearly structured argument? There can be but, as above, let's go for what the examiner is looking for: a clearly structured argument. This is one with signposting throughout, just as we had with our earlier argument on home education.

Now let's look for any differences between the two versions:
- no mention of relevance in instructions on paper
- no reference to the need for a 'convincing' argument on paper
- no reference to the issue of assumptions on paper

We can safely ignore the first two points of difference. It seems pretty obvious that you need to write a 'relevant' argument, one that's on the subject. The term 'convincing' is an oddity not worth spending much time on. It would rule out bizarre reasoning such as, 'Since the Martians landed and banned home education of Earthling children…' 'Convincing' is a very difficult criterion to use, in that what may convince one person may not convince another. So let's forget about 'convincing'. It's a criterion that is largely impossible to apply.

The third difference, though, is worth a serious mention. What does it mean?

Look at the next example. It's an excerpt from an argument that is used to give guidance to examiners on how to award marks. In this case, the argument is given as one which gets full marks. It has to have the conclusion 'We need to rehabilitate offenders rather than punish them.' Here's part of the reasoning:

Rehabilitating prisoners allows them to learn new skills which they can use to find a job when they leave prison…

Just think about this reason. Does it not require at least two assumptions?
- Jobs are available for ex-prisoners.
- The level of skills taught in prison education is high enough to help ex-prisoners get jobs.

Further reasoning in the argument includes the following:

Drug addicts could reform and get clean, thanks to rehabilitating them and showing them what effects their drug-taking has on others…

Once again, we can find some assumptions are needed here:

- Knowing the effects of drug-taking on others will reduce the risk of re-offending.
- These people committed crime as a result of drug addiction.
- Rehabilitation will act to stop drug addicts returning to drug-taking (and thus crime) when they have left prison.

So we've found five assumptions in this argument without even looking for any more in the rest of it.

What this tells us is that you should pay little attention to this requirement in the mark scheme. I doubt if there's an examiner in the land who could operate it without problems. This is because, of course, even really well structured, well reasoned arguments will contain many assumptions. So just write your argument, with its reasons and conclusions, and everything else without giving a thought to this aspect of the mark scheme.

There is also the point about the need for good 'grammar, spelling and punctuation'. There was reliable talk that not too long ago every candidate for a critical thinking paper was simply given the top band mark for these three things. Well, why not? It's unlikely that you wouldn't be seen as being at least competent in doing these. For example, you wouldn't write, 'At least one reason, is given', would you?

So let's pull this together:
- To score well, your argument needs to have a clear structure (signposting in some form will help here) with at least three reasons.
- An intermediate conclusion will be drawn from probably two of these, with the third one supporting the main conclusion via a different route.
- A counter-position will be given in some form, together with some evidence (including the use of examples).
- The main conclusion will be clearly stated and will be accurate in terms of what you are meant to be arguing for or against. For example, if you were asked to argue against the conclusion 'Home education should not be allowed,' then the counter-conclusion has to be 'Home education should be allowed' and not something like 'Home education is a good thing.'

We can now apply all of this to a question based on the general area of the material we've been using for the earlier questions.

Consider the following claim: 'People should ensure that what they eat doesn't contribute to damaging the planet.'

Some people might say that what's on their plate couldn't possibly make any difference to the health of the planet. Individuals can't make any difference to what's sold for food, they will say. But although this argument might make sense at one level, it doesn't when we start adding up what large numbers of individuals eat. Everyone who eats fish contributes to the catching of fish. Nobody would go out and catch fish if individuals weren't asking them to do it by buying the fish they bring back.

The decline of marine life is very disturbing. Given that fish could disappear from the world's seas and oceans by 2050, this would mean that the seas and oceans would no longer work as an ecosystem. The majority of the planet is water, so if the ecosystem of the oceans wasn't functioning, then the ecosystem of the world wouldn't function.

But of course, it's not just fish. It's also meat. The huge amounts of energy required to produce meat are a big contributor to global warming. And the methane gas that comes in large volumes from animals farmed for meat (especially cattle and sheep) is a big contributor to the problem of what are called greenhouse gases.

So if everyone thought more carefully about what they eat, many of the problems likely to affect the planet would be reduced. Therefore people should ensure that what they eat doesn't contribute to damaging the planet.

> This, as you can see, should bring a smile to the face of even the most stern-faced examiner. It's got the lot. Let's show it again, detailing the sequence of the argument.

(CA) Some people might say that what's on their plate couldn't possibly make any difference to the health of the planet. Individuals can't make any difference to what's sold for food, they will say.

(R1) Nobody would go out and catch fish if individuals weren't asking them to do it by buying the fish they bring back.

(IC1) Everyone who eats fish contributes to the catching of fish.

(IC2) (Thus) although this (counter-) argument might make sense at one level, it doesn't when we start adding up what large numbers of individuals eat.

(R2) Given that fish could disappear from the world's seas and oceans by 2050, this would mean that the seas and oceans would no longer work as an ecosystem.

(R3) The majority of the planet is water.

(IC3) So if the ecosystem of the oceans wasn't functioning, then the ecosystem of the world wouldn't function. (A hypothetical IC.)

(IC4) The decline of marine life is very disturbing.

(R4) The huge amounts of energy required to produce meat are a big contributor to global warming.

(R5, including evidence/example) And the methane gas that comes in large volumes from animals farmed for meat (especially cattle and sheep) is a big contributor to the problem of what are called greenhouse gases.

(IC5) It's not just fish (that's a problem), it's also meat.

(IC6) So if everyone thought more carefully about what they eat, many of the problems likely to affect the planet would be reduced.

(C) Therefore people should ensure that what they eat doesn't contribute to damaging the planet.

> You might think that this is a little over the top with its five reasons and six interme-diate conclusions. But it should show you that writing an argument with plenty of

intermediate conclusions isn't that amazing. You'll probably find that as you plan your argument, the ICs just keep emerging from the way in which you develop your argument.

So what does an argument that attracts one of the middling marks look like?

Too many people are eating too much fish, which is going to leave the world's oceans and seas without fish. They don't seem to realise that this will be bad for the planet. Some deep-sea fish take a very long time to breed and they're being caught before they can. People just seem to eat what they like without caring. They should care. If they don't, they'll make the problem worse. People shouldn't damage the planet when they eat.

This is clearly an argument related to the claim. But it suffers from a lack of development and careful organisation.

The first sentence starts well, by giving a reason. But then things get somewhat less clear. The second sentence could be seen as an additional reason, but it doesn't fit well within a structure in this way. The third sentence might be evidence or a further reason. The fourth could well be a reason, but going where? The fifth ('They should care') supports the conclusion in the last sentence. The hypothetical in the sixth sentence is another reason. The conclusion follows but it isn't expressed as it should be, given the claim in the question.

So it's all a bit directionless. There's no rhythm, no sequence to delight us. At around 5 marks, not bad, but we could have done so much better.

Well, that's it. Another 30 marks to add to the 45 already awarded — an A grade.